# SCIENCE TREASURES
Let's Repeat The Great Experiments

## OTHER BOOKS BY BOB BROWN

*Science Circus*

*Science Circus #2*

*Science and You*

# SCIENCE TREASURES
Let's Repeat The Great Experiments

by

Bob Brown

FLEET PRESS CORPORATION

New York

© Copyright 1968 FLEET PRESS CORPORATION

All rights reserved

Library of Congress Catalogue Card Number: 68-23980

Manufactured in the United States of America

No portion of this book may be reprinted in any form without the written permission of the publisher, except by a reviewer who wishes to quote brief passages in connection with a review for a newspaper, magazine, or radio-television program.

*To my grandchildren*

*Kurt, Cindy, Gwen and Lisa*

INTRODUCTION

Have you ever wondered how scientists who lived centuries ago made such startling scientific discoveries and inventions? To satisfy the curiosity of interested students of science, both young and old, *Science Treasures*, skillfully leads the reader through the ages helping him to share in both the problems and successes of geniuses such as Aristotle, Galileo Galilei, Isaac Newton, and many others.

This book is a logical sequel to the popular and successful *Science Circus* books previously written by Mr. Brown. Outstanding experiments conducted by famous scientists have been described with such clarity that the elementary or junior high school student can easily perform many of them, thereby extending his understanding and appreciation of science.

The scientist is described as a "believable" human being who experienced failures and successes while he questioned old beliefs and sought to discover new truths. Many of the problems described are still encountered by twentieth century boys and girls as they attempt to unravel the mysteries of science. Descriptions of important political, social, and religious events associated with the scientists life and work vividly portray the interrelationship between science and the humanities.

The many thousands of students and teachers who have heard Mr. Brown in person will want this book for their own. It is a book which will prove to be highly popular in all libraries and classrooms frequented by young people. In teacher education programs *Science Treasures* will have practical value for students in laboratory oriented science education courses on the university level.

                        A. Paul Wishart, Ph.D.
                        Professor of Science Education
                        University of Tennessee
                        Knoxville, Tennessee

# CONTENTS

| | |
|---|---|
| Aristotle<br>384-322 B.C. | 1 |
| Archimedes<br>287-212 B.C. | 6 |
| Petrus Peregrinus<br>Circa 1269 | 12 |
| Leonardo da Vinci<br>1452-1519 | 16 |
| Galileo Galilei<br>1564-1642 | 24 |
| Otto Van Guericke<br>1602-1686 | 34 |
| Robert Hooke<br>1635-1703 | 38 |
| Isaac Newton<br>1642-1727 | 43 |
| Daniel Bernoulli<br>1700-1782 | 54 |
| Benjamin Franklin<br>1706-1790 | 64 |
| Joseph Priestley<br>1733-1854 | 76 |

# CONTENTS

| | |
|---|---|
| Alessandro Volta<br>1745-1827 | 81 |
| William Henry<br>1774-1836 | 93 |
| Rene Laënnec<br>1781-1826 | 97 |
| Michael Faraday<br>1791-1867 | 107 |
| Joseph Henry<br>1799-1878 | 115 |
| William Thomson, Lord Kelvin<br>1824-1907 | 126 |
| Antoine Becquerel<br>1852-1908 | 135 |
| Nikola Tesla<br>1856-1943 | 140 |
| *Index* | 160 |

# Aristotle
## 384-322 B.C.

Many of the great experiments of science can be repeated easily, and many of them are included in this book. Let us begin with an experiment that today is known to be unscientific, unsound, and untrue. Rather, it is an observation that made up a small part of a great man's adverse influence in physics, an influence that lasted fifteen hundred years!

Aristotle was born in Stagira, Greece. His father, an educated man, was court physician to the grandfather of Alexander the Great, and saw to it that his son received a good education at home. At seventeen, Aristotle was sent to Athens to study under Plato, one of the great Greek philosophers.

Aristotle did not always agree with Plato. He chose to use his great ability to think, reason, inquire, and explore. Soon he began to investigate the wonderful world of biology, and in these investigations he employed the true scientific principle. He sent men to all parts of the known world to collect samples, to classify, and to learn everything possible about the plants and animals.

He was tutor to Alexander, the boy who became Alexander the Great, and it was this young leader who provided Aristotle with money to conduct his searches, researches, and experiments.

In physics Aristotle considered himself a great world authority, but he did not engage in any experimenting in this field. He sought to explain physical phenomena by reasoning power alone. For example when a green log of wood burned on a fire, he observed that water oozed, smoke came out, fire was produced, and ashes were left.

So, he reasoned, there must be five elements in the universe: fire, water, earth (the ashes), and air (the smoke—and a fifth, of which the heavens were made, an element unchanging and everlasting.

The heavens traveled in a circular motion, he said, therefore the circle was a perfect figure. Centuries later, when Johannes Kepler (1571–1630) found that the planets travel not in circles but in ellipses, he had great difficulty convincing the scientists of his day that his findings were correct.

In this, as in other teachings, scientists could not believe that the great Aristotle could be wrong. This blind worship of Aristotle continued, in greater or less degree, for a century and a half.

Aristotle wrote that the heavier a body is, the faster it falls. He knew that a leaf falls more slowly than a stone. He did not take the trouble to find out by experiment whether two stones of different weights would fall at the same or different speeds. He thought it reasonable that a heavier body falls faster, and taught this fallacy to his pupils.

He made many such errors, and scientists believed his statements without question. Scientists who dared to suspect that Aristotle could be wrong were often open to ridicule.

Aristotle produced between four hundred and a thousand books. At one time he is said to have had a thousand men working for him, helping to compile his works on the biological sciences. It is not known how many of the books he himself wrote. Perhaps he wrote some and simply compiled the others from the writings of his scientific investigators, but in any case Aristotle deserves much credit. The writing was magnificent.

He was a great biological scientist. It is regrettable that his teachings on matters physical were not equally sound.

Aristotle saw a log of green wood burning on a fire, with water oozing out, flames showing, smoke curling upward, and ashes accumulating beneath. So, he reasoned, there must be four elements on earth: fire, water, earth, and air. This is a classical example of unscientific science.

# Archimedes
## 287-212 B.C.

Archimedes is sometimes called the first great inventor, and yet he did not want to be remembered for his inventions but rather for his mathematical discoveries.

We are not certain about many details of his life. His birth date probably was 287 B.C. He may have been related to King Hiero; we do know they were great friends. It is believed that he was sent to school at Alexandria, the intellectual capital of the world, when he was eleven years old.

He was born at Syracuse, on the island of Sicily, and what we know of his life is bound up with this city. He is thought to be the discoverer of the principles of levers and pulleys, and this is enough to give him everlasting fame. But he did much more.

When he discovered the principle of the lever he boasted: "Give me a place to stand, and a fulcrum, and I can move the world." His friend the king challenged him to prove his boast by moving some great weight.

It happened that King Hiero had built a ship for King Ptolemy, and all the efforts of all the men who worked on it failed to move it into the water.

Here was just the kind of test that pleased the young genius. He built a system of pulleys and ropes, attached them to the ship, then allowed the king himself to pull the end of the rope. Without too much effort the king pulled the ship into the water.

Then came another test of Archimedes' genius. The king had just received a new crown from his goldsmith and wanted to be certain that the smith had not added some base metal to the gold. He assigned to Archimedes the task of finding out, but warned him that the crown must not be broken or bent.

This was a problem indeed! Archimedes pondered for many days. One day at the baths he sank down into his tub and noticed that the water overflowed and that his weight seemed to diminish to nothing. Suddenly the solution to the riddle flashed into his mind. According to legend he forgot to dress, and ran into the street shouting *"Eureka!"*—A Greek word that means "I've found it!"

He had made a great discovery. He could show the king how much water would overflow from a vessel filled to the brim when a piece of pure gold weighing exactly as much as the crown was submerged. He could then refill the vessel, submerge the crown, and if more water overflowed this time it would prove that a baser, lighter, metal had been combined with the gold in the making of the crown.

The test was made. It showed that a lighter metal had been added. The goldsmith confessed and was put to death.

The one device that bears his name today is the

Archimedes pump or screw. This he invented for pumping water out of a ship's hold. It is a spiral-shaped tube which turns on a cylinder, lifting the water as the turns appear to rise. Two kinds of Archimedes' screws are attributed to him; we do not know which kind he actually used. The devices are still used for pumping water in some Asiatic countries.

Archimedes discovered many truths of mathematics. He came very near discovering the calculus, and no doubt would have, except that the Greeks did not have number characters such as we have today. They had no cipher and knew nothing of decimals or algebra.

His most spectacular accomplishments were his inventions of war machines. When Marcellus and the Romans besieged his city, Syracuse, he devised catapults that hurled huge stones to wreck the enemy ships. He built cranes with giant claws that lifted the ships from the water and overturned them.

Legend has it that he built concave mirrors that focused the sun's rays on the ships, setting them afire, but many do not believe this. However, he kept the Romans at bay for two years with his inventions. Marcellus gave up the fight, concluding that the only way to take the city was to starve its people into surrender. This he did. But he had great respect for the man who had made his war tasks so difficult, and gave orders that Archimedes, his home, and his relatives be spared.

But as the bloodthirsty soldiers sacked the fallen city one of them came upon Archimedes, now quite elderly, engrossed in a mathematical problem. Ordered to come to Marcellus, Archimedes told the soldier to wait. The soldier, infuriated, thrust his sword into the body of the scholar.

Marcellus was grieved at the deed and did what he could to comfort Archimedes' relatives. He gave him an honorable burial, and marked his grave with the emblem Archimedes had requested be used: a cylinder circumscribing a sphere, chosen because he had proved by elementary methods that the volume of a sphere inscribed in a cylinder so that the sphere touched the sides and ends of the cylinder was just two thirds the volume of the cylinder. The formula for the volume of a cylinder was known, and thus he deduced the formula for the volume of a sphere.

He was justifiably proud of this mathematical accomplishment.

A model of Archimedes' screw is easy to make, as shown in the photograph. A wooden rolling pin is used as the cylinder. A crank made of coat-hanger wire is attached to the upper end, and part of the handle at the lower end is sawed off to let the hose go deeper into the water. A wire support holds the upper end of the rolling pin and the lower end turns in a depression made in a lead paper weight.

As the crank is turned, the lower end of the hose scoops up water and raises it as the turns themselves seem to rise. The water pours out at the upper end of the hose with every turn of the crank.

This is probably the kind of screw Archimedes used, although another type, made of a screw fitted within a pipe, is also attributed to him.

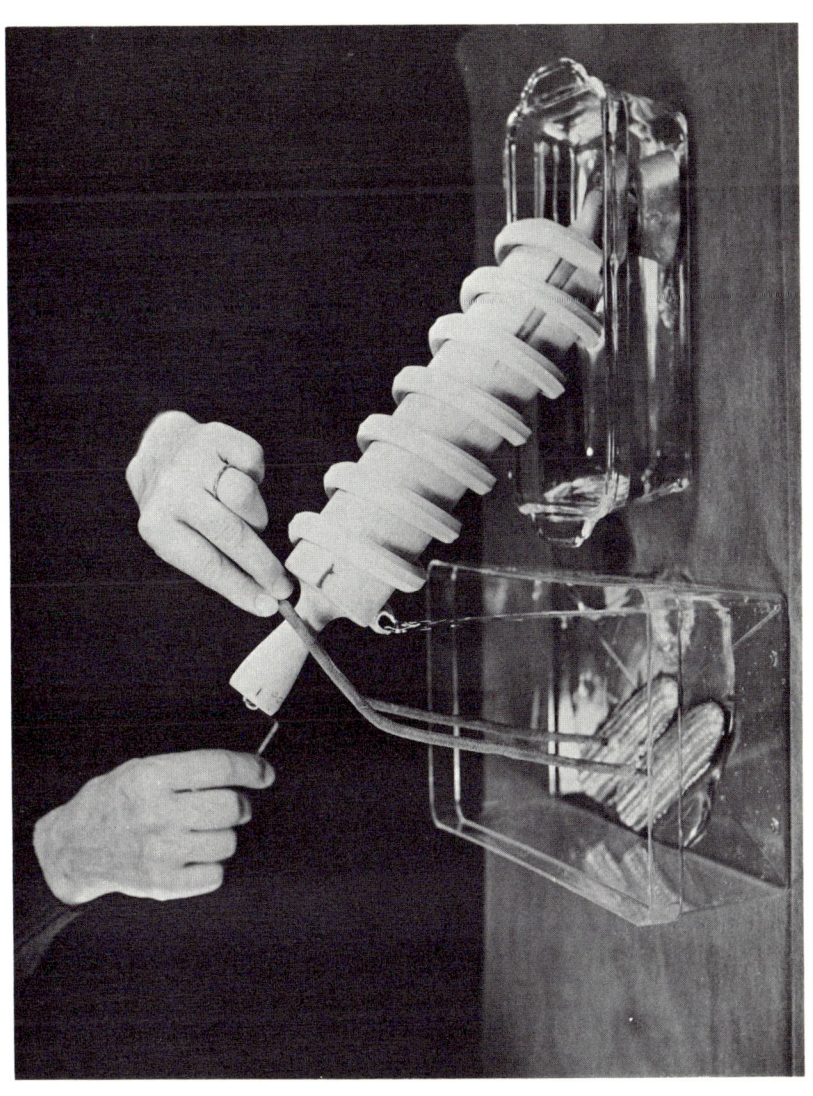

# Petrus Peregrinus
## (date unknown)

One man's search for a method of "perpetual motion" led to the scientific investigation of magnets, probably the first.

Perpetual motion was the impossible dream of many men in the past. Clever machines were made, numerous ideas were spawned, and much time and money were spent in this quest before scientists finally learned that no machine, once started, could run forever without having energy added in some way.

Petrus Peregrinus had such a dream. We know very little about him—not even when he was born or when he died, except that he was convinced that perpetual motion could be achieved with magnets.

He probably studied at the University of Paris and served in the engineering corps of the French army. In a letter he told a friend about his discoveries. He then was in the army in 1269.

He used the word "pole" for the first time in regard to magnets. He described how a north pole attracts a south pole and how two like poles repel. He told how, if a magnet is broken, it becomes two magnets, each with its own north and south poles.

He put a magnet on a pivot, with a graduated circle around it, to make what was probably the first compass as we know it today. Formerly, the magnets in compasses were floated on a liquid.

It is easy to perform the Peregrinus broken-magnet experiment. First, magnetize a sewing needle by rubbing one end of it on one end of a permanent magnet. Next, wrap the magnetized needle in a handkerchief, for protection as the needle breaks. Break the needle in the handkerchief. You will find that both pieces of the needle are complete magnets, each with its own north and south poles.

# Leonardo da Vinci
## 1452-1519

Would you believe that the artist who painted the most famous picture in the world was also one of the world's greatest scientists and inventors?

This was Leonardo da Vinci, the creator of the painting *La Gioconda*, commonly known as the *Mona Lisa*.

He invented the parachute, the helicopter, the turbine engine, a variable speed drive something like that used in automobiles, a projector, a lens grinder, a pulley system, aerial bombs, machine guns, submarines, bridges, canal locks, diggers, a printing press, an air conditioner, a lifting jack, roller bearings, a pump, a power saw, a cannon, a ship's hull, a clock, a revolving stage—and this is only the beginning of the list.

He did not live to see many of his inventions used, and many people of his day thought him just a little crazy. You see, this was even before Columbus sailed to America.

His father, Piero da Vinci, was a prominent notary and lawyer in the little village of Vinci. His mother, Caterina, was a peasant girl. Soon after his birth he was taken to live with his wealthy grandparents, who gave him all that a young boy needs in the way of food, home, and education. He did not always agree, however, with their ideas and wishes for his education. They thought he should be a lawyer, but young Leonardo was bored by such notions.

His father saw that the boy had talent in painting, and showed some of his son's drawings to a great Florentine artist of the day, Andrea del Verrocchio (1435–1488). The artist, recognizing talent, was delighted to take Leonardo as a pupil.

His studies included painting, sculpture, and engineering. By the time he was twenty his work was so good that he was admitted to the painters' guild of Florence. He left Verrocchio when he was twenty-five, and from then until he was thirty he lived well, fulfilling commissions for paintings. He had a house, servants, and horses.

Leonardo boasted of his accomplishments in a letter of application for a job in 1481, written to Ludovico Sforza, the ruler of Milan, who was threatened by powerful military forces of Venice, Rome, and France. He wrote:

1. I could build light bridges, easily moved, and heavy bridges to resist attack and be raised and lowered. I could burn and destroy enemy bridges.

2. For attack, I could drain moats and build scaling ladders.

3. To defeat strong enemies, I could carry out mining operations.

4. I could make cannon, easily transported, to shoot burning matter. The smoke would cause terror and confusion.

5. I could tunnel noiselessly under enemy walls, and even under rivers.

6. I could build strong covered wagons to carry guns into enemy lines and clear a safe path for infantry.

7. I could make cannon, mortars, and engines of fire different from those in use.

8. I could build catapults and other "projecting weapons" not yet known.

9. I could build ships gunproof and fireproof and engines of great power for attack and defense.

10. I could, in times of peace, compete with anyone in architecture, sculpture, and painting—and build canals.

He stressed his usefulness in war, and only in the last item did he mention his artistic talents. He added that he could build a bronze horse in memory of Sforza's father, and offered to demonstrate any of his abilities in a park.

The letter was written after Leonardo learned that Sforza was looking for someone to build the horse. After some delay, he got the job; and although he started the horse and worked on it at times over a period of years, it was never finished.

He was noted for his failure to complete some of his tasks. The great horse was finished in clay, but in this case it was not Leonardo's fault that it was never cast in bronze. War made it necessary that all available bronze be used in making cannon, and the clay horse fell apart in bad weather.

His first great painting, *The Last Supper*, was painted on the wall of a dining room in a monastery. It depicted the scene as Jesus ate his final meal with his disciples. It has been restored several times, and can be seen by visitors today.

Leonardo spent a year traveling with the army

of Cesare Borgia. He drew maps, inspected forts, invented bridges and weapons, and devised the plans for draining marshes.

He was interested in many subjects: anatomy, astronomy, geology, botany, geography, mathematics, mechanics, the chemistry of paints and oils, physics, aviation. He excelled in all. He designed airplanes according to sound principles. One of his models flew a little, and he was almost tried for witchcraft as a result. He had no engines to make large planes fly.

His interest in anatomy was twofold: he needed knowledge of the structure of the human body in his art, and he had enormous curiosity about all things, including the structure of the body. He wanted to know for the sake of knowing—a trait all true scientists share.

Leonardo, casting aside superstition pertaining to the human body, dissected corpses, making exact drawings as he did so. From these drawings doctors learned for the first time the structure of organs and muscles. Leonardo went so far as to build a model of the human heart, which he called a "pump."

He wrote many books. Apparently he planned to classify his thousands of drawings of inventions and mechanical principles, but this was never done.

His life at times was hard. Toward the end, after many failures, he was penniless and scorned. In 1515, Francis I, king of France, invited him to his country to be "first painter and engineer to the king," a post that provided him with a house, a pension, and great honor.

Only four years of this pleasant life remained for him. His eyesight was failing; his hand became paralyzed. He died in France on May 2, 1519, and was buried in the little church of St. Florentine, in Amboise.

Later the grave was dug up and the bones scattered. Nothing remains to mark the last resting place of the greatest artist, inventor, and engineer of his time—or as many believe, the greatest of all time.

Leonardo knew about ball and roller bearings, which he called "friction removers." He suggests, as an experiment, sliding a weight, noting that the friction varies with the smoothness of the surfaces that touch.

Then, he says, move the weight upon balls on a smooth surface, and "see that it will move without effort." This statement is a slight exaggeration, since there is some effort involved.

Da Vinci drew plans for a parachute, but whether he ever made one is doubtful. He said: "If a man have a tent made of linen of which the apertures have all been stopped up, and it be twelve braccia across and twelve in depth, he will be able to throw himself down from any great height without suffering any injury." The quotation is from the brochure "Leonardo da Vinci," published by International Business Machines.

An easy way to show the action of ball bearings in reducing friction is shown in the photo. Use two paint cans, place marbles in the depressions around the rim of one and set the other down on top of it. The upper can turns easily. Try it without the marbles and see the difference.

It is easy to make a parachute with a handkerchief, string, and weight. Throw it upward so that the weight pushes the cloth up. As it comes down the cloth opens out, and because of wind resistance its downward speed is held to a graceful minimum.

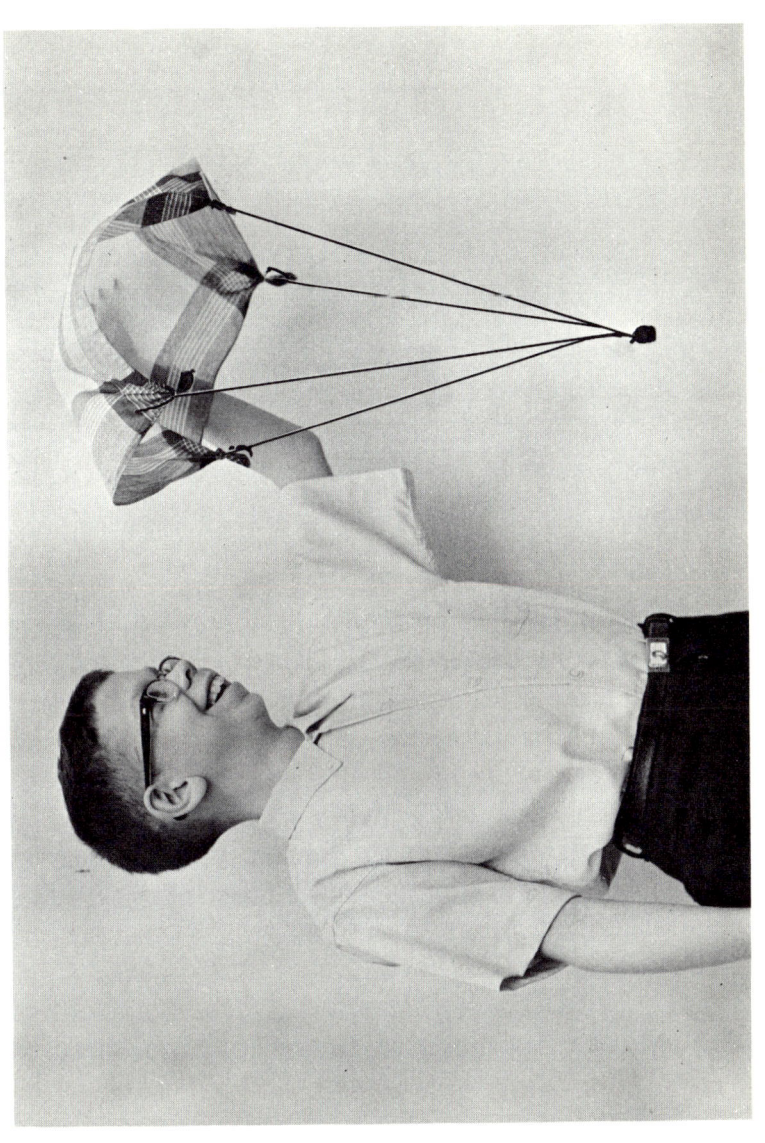

## *Galileo Galilei*
## *1564-1642*

The church has often opposed advances in science, and even today this is true in some localities. One of the most tragic instances of the suffering of a scientist at the hands of the church is seen in the life story of Galileo Galilei.

The church was not alone in its opposition to new ideas. The professors of the period were themselves sometimes enemies of science. They clung to the beliefs and teachings of Aristotle as blindly as the clerics clung to the "facts" as related in holy writ. They were willing to persecute anyone who doubted, although they did not resort to the physical tortures of the Inquisition as did their contemporaries who considered themselves the representatives of God.

Galileo was born in Pisa near the Leaning Tower. He had religious inclinations, and wanted to be a priest. He was placed in the hands of the monks of Vallambrosa for training and probably would have remained there but for an inflammation of the eyes. When the disorder did not respond to treatment, the boy's father, Vincenzio Galilei, removed him from the monastery.

The father was the leading lute player of Italy, a composer of music, and a prominent mathematician. There was little money in these accomplishments, and for that reason he did not want his son to be either a musician or mathematician. He wanted young Galileo to be a cloth merchant.

The Galilei family belonged to the nobility, and it was thought necessary that formal learning be given to young Galileo, who surprised everyone by his ability to learn rapidly. So the father changed his mind and decided that the study of medicine would be appropriate for his son. Doctors made a good deal of money. At seventeen years of age Galileo entered the University of Pisa to study medicine.

At eighteen he made his first important discovery. While watching the swinging lamp in the Cathedral of Pisa, fascinated by its behavior, he found that the time of the swing, regardless of the length of the oscillation, was always the same. His experiments which followed resulted in his law of the pendulum, a law that is still taught today.

Galileo, like all people, scientists included, was sometimes wrong. At about this period of his life he made one of his mistakes. In trying to explain the lifting of water by a pump, he erred by quoting the old saying, "Nature abhors a vacuum." The real reason is that the water is pushed up by the pressure of the atmosphere.

He discovered by accident, through a friend, the beauty of mathematics, and despite his father's wishes he began to study geometry. He absorbed Euclid and Archimedes with great pleasure in remarkably short time. Possibly his father felt a secret pride in his son, though money was not in it; mathematicians are kindred spirits, after all.

His education did not stop when, at twenty-one, his father's money was gone and he had to leave school. His investigation of the laws of nature and science increased. He drew the attention of the savants of the day with a water balance he invented, and intrigued them with a paper he wrote on the center of gravity in solids.

As he delved deeper he became more and more convinced that the great Aristotle had made mistakes. Aristotle had declared that the speed of a falling body is in direct proportion to its weight, that a ten-pound weight such as a stone would fall ten times faster than a one-pound stone. No one had ever doubted this before; it had been taught since Aristotle first said it, and all accepted it as a fact. Galileo experimented and found it to be false.

He gathered the learned professors together at the Leaning Tower, climbed to the top of the 181-foot overhang, from which he simultaneously dropped two unequal weights—a stone of one hundred pounds and the other weighing one pound. Both struck the ground together.

Yet this did not make him popular and respected. The professors were not convinced; they laughed at him at every opportunity. Their ridicule drove him away to Florence, where he lived without a job or money. A further calamity—his father died, leaving three sisters and a brother, all younger, for Galileo to look after.

He appealed to a rich and powerful friend, Marchese Guidubalde del Monte of Pesaro, who was able to get him a job as lecturer at the University of Padua. His contract was for six years, at $200 a year—a very good salary at that time.

Galileo visited the romantic city of Venice, and there he fell in love. He never married his beloved, but he provided her with a home, and she presented him with three children. She later married someone else, with Galileo's blessing, and in 1599 Galileo was re-elected to his position at the University for another six years, with a salary increase to $350 a year. Galileo was happy and prosperous.

But trouble was coming. Aristotle had taught that the earth was the center of the universe and that the sun, moon, and stars revolved around it. A new star appeared in the sky in 1609. Galileo began to talk about it, going so far as to declare that Copernicus (A.D. 1473–1543) was right, that the earth revolves around the sun.

Galileo declared that the heavens are not fixed and unchanging, that here was a new star to prove it. But the professors again were unconvinced; once more they heaped abuse on the young scientist who dared to disagree with Aristotle.

Hans Lippershey, at Middelburg in the Netherlands, discovered about this time that if he put two lenses together he could produce a fine toy—something that would make distant objects seem nearer. Galileo immediately made use of the idea by constructing a telescope. So pleased were his superiors at this accomplishment that they doubled his salary at Padua and assured him of his position for the rest of his life.

He built more lenses and telescopes, and saw that the moon is not smooth, but pock-marked and mountainous. He announced that the Milky Way is made up of countless stars. The professors did not believe; Aristotle had not said such things. When Galileo observed that Jupiter has two moons, it was just too much for them.

Church people were horrified. This star-gazer just must be stopped, they insisted. He was destroying the religion of the people with discoveries that did not conform to the teachings of the Scriptures. Galileo decided to go to Rome, to make sure that his discoveries had not offended the Pope, and there he was received with honor, but with a warning.

He was forbidden henceforth to teach that the world is round and revolves around the sun.

Years passed. Galileo was sixty now, and a new Pope was enthroned. He thought it safe to publish a book on the motion of the stars and planets. However, his enemies were waiting for just such an act; the ban on his teaching of the Copernican system had not been lifted. He was ordered back to Rome.

This time there were no honors. He was ordered to prison to await the Inquisition's verdict. He must publicly admit that he was wrong or else endure horrible torture. Days and weeks passed. We do not know how far the inquisitors had to go to get the feeble old man to sign his name to a statement admitting heresy. But he signed.

No longer was he a free man. From that time on he was a prisoner of the church. He was allowed to live outside the prison, and it was his wish that his daughter, Maria Celeste, a nun, might live with him and be his comfort. But the worry over her father's ordeal at the hands of the Inquisition ruined her health and she died.

Work was his only friend now. He was allowed to experiment in mechanics, and his investigations resulted in the book *Dialogue on the New Sciences*, which formulated laws of hydrostatics, of falling bodies, of cohesion, of motion, of acceleration. Some of his facts later became Newton's laws of motion, important and well known to all science students today.

The book was finished in 1636. In 1638 he was incurably blind. One of his last wishes was that he might apply his laws of the pendulum to the making of an instrument for keeping time—a clock. This wish was not fulfilled. He died on the eighth of January, 1642.

One of Galileo's experiments with the pendulum is shown in the drawing of the boy with the weight on a string. If the string is pulled back and allowed to swing free, the weight reaches a certain distance to the right before it begins to swing back.

Now if the weight is pulled back to the same place and allowed to swing free so that the string hits a nail in the wall or other stationary object, the weight will gain speed as the string is stopped by the shelf, but it will go just as high as before. It returns quickly until the string leaves the nail, then it resumes its slower swing back to the starting point.

Another of Galileo's experiments, easy to demonstrate but which did not impress some of the professors of his day, is that of falling bodies. In the drawing, the girl is dropping two cells of battery, one a No. 6 dry cell, the other a flashlight D cell. If they are dropped simultaneously they meet the ground at the same time. In this experiment it is necessary to use two objects of the same density but of different sizes. A small stone and a large one will do, but not a small stone and a large handkerchief. Air resistance on the handkerchief would be too great and would retard its fall.

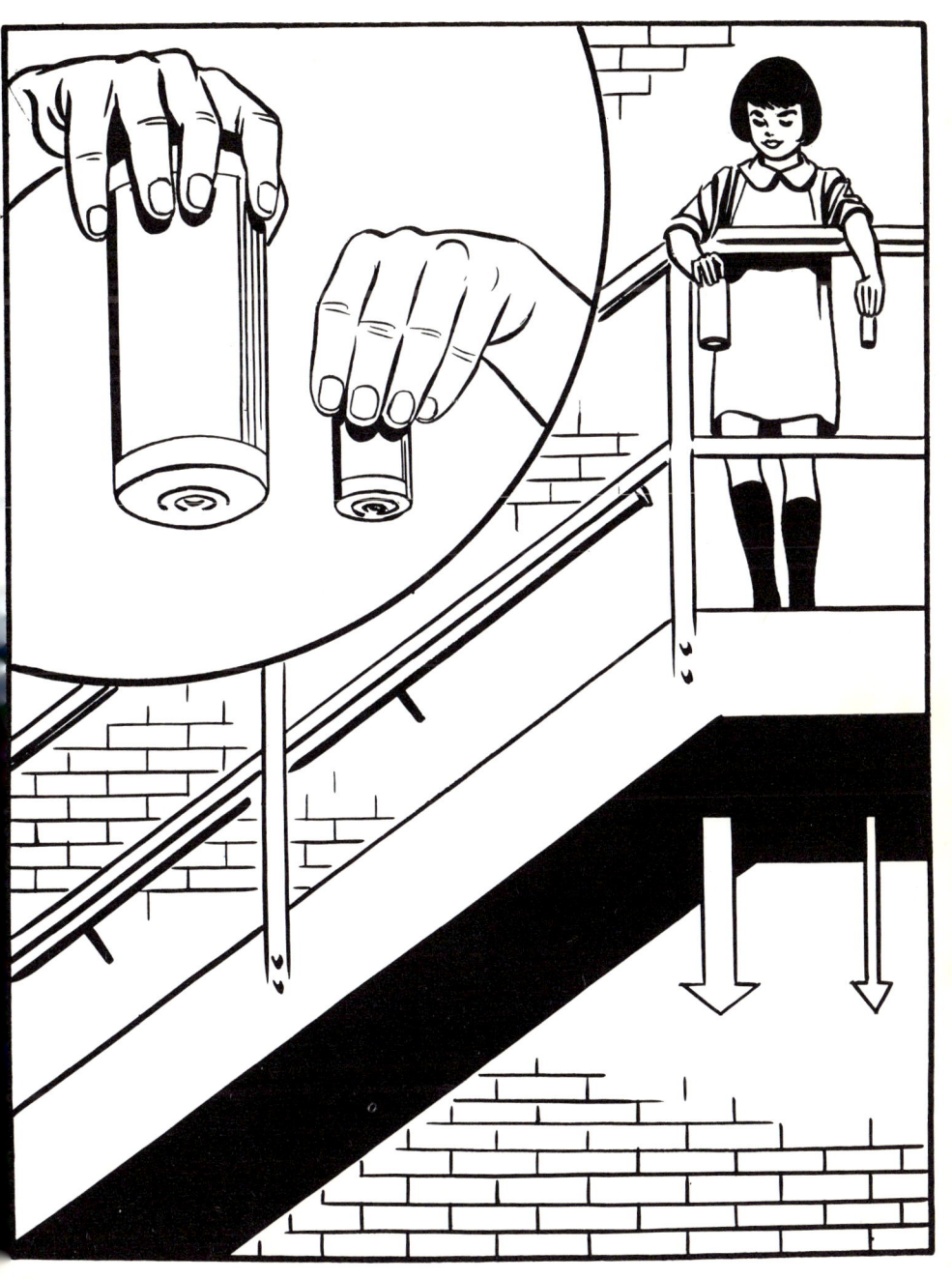

# Otto von Guericke
## 1602-1686

Otto von Guericke, a German natural philosopher (today he would be called a scientist), is best remembered for a scientific experiment (perhaps it could be called a "stunt") performed in 1654, known as the Magdeburg hemispheres.

Otto was born in Magdeburg, in Prussian Saxony, and studied law and mathematics in Germany and Leyden. In 1627 he was elected alderman of Magdeburg. In 1646, he became mayor of Magdeburg and a magistrate of Brandenburg. He took care of his civic duties, in his leisure time devoting himself to science, mainly pneumatics.

He was excited by the discoveries of Galileo, Blaise Pascal (1623–1662), and Evangelista Torricelli (1608–1647), and attempted to create a vacuum. During the time he spent in this effort he invented the air pump in 1650. He dabbled in electrical research, and invented an electric machine. He became interested in astronomy, doing research which led to the means by which astronomers could predict the return of comets.

His Magdeburg hemispheres experiment was performed to demonstrate the pressure of the atmosphere. The story is that he made two hemispheres of brass, three feet in diameter, making the edges airtight and attaching a pipe through which he could pump out air. He smeared the edges with grease to tighten the seal. Two teams of horses were brought and attached, one to each hemisphere. When the air was pumped out, the horses could not pull the hemispheres apart.

No wonder. If the hemispheres had been only one foot in diameter, the atmosphere pressing on them could have held them together with a force of a ton.

In this and other experiments von Guericke showed for the first time that it was possible to pump air as though it were water.

The pressure of the air in which we live is expressed in surprisingly large figures. For example, the air pressure on a floor 12 by 15 feet is about 190 tons. The pressure is exerted from all sides, including both top and bottom, so the floor is not crushed.

The pressure of the atmosphere is 14.7 pounds per square inch. This means that if we could have a tube one inch square reaching to the upper limits of the atmosphere, the air in it would weigh 14.7 pounds.

It is interesting to note that von Guericke was a showman as well as a scientist. He used two teams of horses, pulling against each other. He could have done the same thing, mechanically, by using one team and tying the other hemisphere to a big tree. The pull would have been the same. But *two* teams looked more impressive.

His famous hemispheres experiment can be repeated easily with two of the rubber plungers known as plumbers' helpers. Wet the edges to provide a tight seal, push them together, then have two strong boys try to pull them apart. If the plungers are four inches in diameter, and if all the air pressure is outside and none inside, it will take a pull of more than 185 pounds to pull them apart. Of course, it would be impossible to take all the air out of space between the plungers. But they are likely to hold with a force of almost a hundred pounds.

# Robert Hooke
## 1635-1703

Next time you look at your watch, think how clever is the little wheel that turns back and forth, and the hair-spring attached to it. These were invented by Robert Hooke, remembered in science mainly for "Hooke's Law."

Hooke was born on the Isle of Wight, off the south coast of England, the son of a curate who was fairly well off. The father died when Robert was thirteen, and the boy then went to London to become an apprentice to a leading portrait painter.

Robert had two unfortunate factors to contend with early in life. He was physically unattractive and he was always ailing, due to sinus headaches, catarrh, giddiness, indigestion, and insomnia.

He had talent as a painter, but was forced to give up the apprenticeship because the paints and oils made him sick. His father had left him 100 pounds, a considerable amount of money, which enabled him to attend Westminster School and later Oxford.

There he worked his way through as a chorister and a valet to a wealthy resident. In 1655 Robert Boyle (1627–1691) hired him as assistant in his experimental science work, and it was not long before he proved his value by inventing an air pump.

His first publication dealt with observations of surface tension; his first invention of great importance was the balance wheel in watches. Prior to that time the watch mechanism was controlled by a swinging bar, which ticked to and fro and was very inaccurate.

When the Royal Society was chartered in 1662, Hooke was hired as its first curator. His main duty was to set up three or four experiments for each weekly meeting of the distinguished group of scientists. He did this admirably and without pay for two years. It was at this time that he prepared his great book *Micrographia*, published in 1665.

This book alone would have given Hooke a place among the great men of science. It described the first compound microscope, and placed its writer among the foremost founders of the microscopic study of biology. It contained sixty excellent drawings of objects that people of the day had never envisioned before, such as the compound eye of a fly and the structure of feathers. The structure of cells was visible in his microscope, and he made drawings of them.

He studied light, crystals, and the craters on the moon, and while not all of his explanations were accurate, they were surprisingly good. He was the best instrument maker of his time, and after the great fire of London in 1666 he helped his friend Christopher Wren plan the rebuilding of the city. Wren made him city surveyor, a job that paid him an adequate amount.

His health did not improve. He never married, but lived with a niece. Her death in 1687, and the shock of it, contributed to the utter failure of his health, and he died in 1703. His funeral was attended by all the noted Fellows of the Royal Society who were in London at the time, but the grave site has been lost.

Hooke's Law states that if one pound will stretch a spring one inch, two pounds will stretch it two inches, four pounds will stretch it four inches, and so on, within the limits of the spring. Simple, yet important enough to bring a man to fame.

To demonstrate Hooke's Law, suspend a small can on the end of a window-shade spring. Place a wire on the can to serve as a pointer. Have three paper triangles ready. Pour a little water into the can to stretch the spring slightly. Place a triangle on the wall at the end of the pointer wire.

Then pour a measured quantity of water into the can, perhaps three or four ounces. Place another triangle at the pointer wire.

Again pour exactly the same amount of water into the can, place the paper at the point indicated by the wire, and the distance between the center triangle and the upper and lower triangles will be found to be the same.

The law, as it applies here, is: Twice the weight of water stretches the spring twice as far.

# Isaac Newton
## 1642-1727

When Isaac Newton was born on Christmas day in 1642, he was not expected to live. He was so small that his mother said he could be put into a quart-size pitcher. Yet he grew into one of the giants of science.

His father died three months before Isaac was born. When he was two years old his mother married again, and the boy was sent to live with his grandmother on a lonely farm. He went to school and at fourteen returned to live with his mother, whose second husband had died. She wanted her son to be a farmer, but as he had no taste for farm life, she allowed him to prepare for college. He entered Trinity College, Cambridge, at eighteen, and at twenty-six he became a professor of mathematics.

An epidemic of bubonic plague closed the university, whereupon he returned once again to his mother's farm. He stayed eighteen months, and during that time discovered, worked out, and planned practically all the great scientific ideas that made him famous.

A falling apple in the garden at his home (according to his own notes) led him to the formulation of his inverse square law of gravitation. He did not have to be hit on the head with the apple. The law states that all bodies in the universe attract each other with a force directly proportional to the product of their masses and inversely to the square of the distance between them.

Scientist and writer W. M. Woods, of Oak Ridge, Tennessee, has an interesting story to tell about this.

"The episode of the apple is much misquoted," he says. "Newton tells it in his own words. It was not the simple fact of the apple's falling. Others before Newton had called the force that makes things fall 'gravity.' Newton saw the apple fall. He then postulated that the force that made it fall extended to the top of the tree, and then speculated whether it 'might not extend higher than the height of the tree, even to the moon.' He then considered whether this force, diminished by the distance, was sufficient to balance the 'centrifugal force' due to the moon's motion. He calculated and found 'it answered tolerably well.' "

Newton could not prove his theory with the existing mathematics. He set about to invent the differential calculus, and to expand the known formulas into the integral calculus. This was a feat which was enough to place him at the head of the list of the great mathematicians of the world.

During that eighteen-month period he began his thinking and experimenting on light. First, he knew that all telescopes were faulty; they gave images with fringes of color around them. He then invented a telescope with a reflector and lens instead of two lenses. Some of today's best telescopes are built on this principle. Next, he experimented with a prism. He let a spot of sunlight come into his darkened room through a hole in a shutter, and as the light went through the prism it was split into the colors of the rainbow. He had discovered that white light is a mixture of colors. Using a second prism, he put the colors back together to get white light. He made one of his new telescopes for the Royal Society of London, which so pleased the members that they elected him a Fellow of the Royal Society, one of the highest honors for a scientist in England. He was thirty years old.

His laws of motion are among his most important contributions to science. His first law states that an object in motion moves in a straight line and at a constant speed unless influenced by a force. For example, a rowboat will continue to move on the water in a straight line unless slowed down by friction or pushed into a different course by an outside force.

The second law states that an outside force acting on an object moves the object in the direction of the force. Example: a force moving east and acting on the boat will tend to make the boat go in an easterly direction.

The third law is the one by which our space rockets move into orbit. It says that for every action there is an equal and opposite reaction. And again, if we use the boat as an example: someone standing at the rear of the boat jumps off, toward the shore. He moves toward the shore, but at the same time the boat moves in the opposite direction.

Newton spent most of his life in controversy with other scientists who discounted his theories and discoveries. He finally left the field of science for a job as master of the mint. Even there he continued to use his brain as a scientist and engineer to improve the process for the minting of coins.

In 1703 he was elected president of the Royal Society and in 1705 was knighted by Queen Anne. He remained president until his death in 1727, at the age of eighty-five, and was buried in Westminster Abbey.

One of his controversies was with Baron Gottfried von Leibnitz (1646–1716), a German philosopher, mathematician, and statesman who invented the fundamental principles of infinitesimal calculus in 1675. Neither he nor Newton knew of the other's work. Newton invented his system of calculus in 1666.

Through his life Newton was occasionally accused of being arrogant, of lacking humility. But one of his statements would show him to be humble and appreciative of the work of others. He said, "If I have seen further it is by standing on the shoulders of giants."

With a spot of sunlight entering a darkened room, Newton used a prism to show that each color is refracted at a different angle, making a "rainbow." He tried a mirror, found that all colors reflected from it at the same angle, which led him to build a telescope using a mirror to replace a lens. Today's best telescopes make use of his mirror discovery.

An easy way to repeat Newton's prism experiment, without a prism, is shown here. A mirror in a pan of water makes a double prism, projecting the rainbow (an imperfect yet beautiful one) on a card.

Newton's third law can be illustrated in many ways. Here a balloon is mounted on a lightweight cart made from Erector wheels and balsa wood. When there is air in the balloon and none comes out, the pressure in the balloon is equal in all directions. If air is allowed to escape toward the rear of the cart, the pressure in that direction is reduced, and the greater pressure toward the front pulls the cart along. The law is: "For every action there is an equal and opposite reaction." In the author's newspaper column "Science For You" this experiment was called "Jet propulsion with a balloon."

Another easy experiment demonstrating Newton's third law is shown here. Make holes in a tin can by driving the nail at an angle. Suspend the can by strings, and as the water comes out of the holes the reaction causes the can to turn and twist the string.

Still a third way of showing Newton's third law is shown here. A piece of metal cut from a coffee can is mounted on a piece of wood as shown. Screws are used at the lower end; the upper end is held with a wire. The wooden platform rests on soda straws or pencils that roll easily.

When the tennis ball is dropped as shown, it strikes the metal. The curving metal changes the course of the ball, pushing it to the left. The ball pushes back on the metal just as much, and so the platform moves to the right on the rollers.

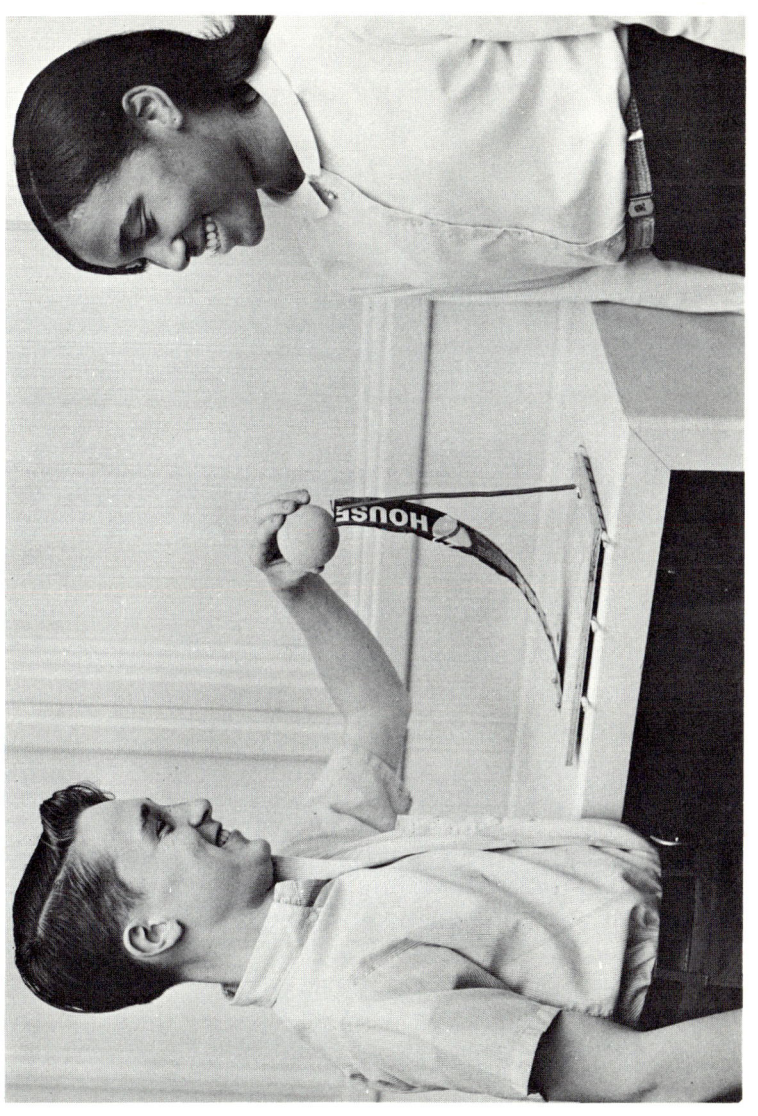

# Daniel Bernoulli
## 1700-1782

A few generations ago the words "phlogiston" and "caloric" were important words in science. They represented errors in the explanation of heat and burning, and this false explanation existed for hundreds of years. One of the first scientists to suggest the correct explanation of heat was the same man who is most noted for his work which led to the success of the airplane.

His name was Daniel Bernoulli, and he was one of a family of geniuses in mathematics and science. Originally from Belgium, the family moved to Switzerland to escape religious persecution. Jakob and his brother Johann were professors of mathematics in Basel. Another brother, Nikolaus, taught mathematics at the Academy in St. Petersburg. Johann's three sons were all mathematicians. One of them, Daniel, was best known.

He was a professor at St. Petersburg, returning to Basel in 1732. He became, at different times, professor of botany, anatomy, and physics. It was in 1738 that Daniel expressed the opinion that the thermometer measures vibrations or movement in solids, liquids, and gases.

The scientists before him had taught that heat is a material substance of some sort, and that when a piece of wood burns, the strange substance phlogiston or caloric is given off and is observed as heat. As so often in science, the accepted explanations continued, and almost no one paid attention to Bernoulli's correct explanation. It was not until fifty years later that Benjamin Thompson (Count Rumford, 1753–1814) conducted experiments to prove Bernoulli correct.

Bernoulli's investigation of the properties of gases, and his expression in mathematics of the principles governing the motion of molecules, made possible the explanation of such phenomena as fluid pressure, energy conduction, evaporation, and osmosis.

Bernoulli's theorem, for which he is best known, states that when the speed of a fluid increases, the pressure decreases. This is illustrated by airplanes in flight. The curved upper surface of the wing causes the air passing over it to move faster than the air passing over the straighter lower surface. Therefore, the reduced pressure of the air on the wing's upper surface causes the lift which keeps the plane in the air.

"How the airplane flies" might be the caption of this simple experiment. Hold a strip of paper to the lower lip, blow over the top of it, and it will rise into the air stream. According to the Bernoulli theorem, the moving air over the top of the strip exerts less pressure on it than the still air underneath, and so the pressure under the strip makes it rise.

Best known of the experiments illustrating the Bernoulli theorem is this: Stick a straight pin through a piece of paper, let the pin come down through a thread spool as the paper rests on the top of the spool. Throw the head back, and blow steadily up through the spool. The paper does not blow off, and the head may be lowered, and still the paper does not blow off as long as the breath is blown steadily.

Air comes out around the hole, between the paper and the spool, and since it is in motion it exerts less pressure than the still air pressing on the top of the paper.

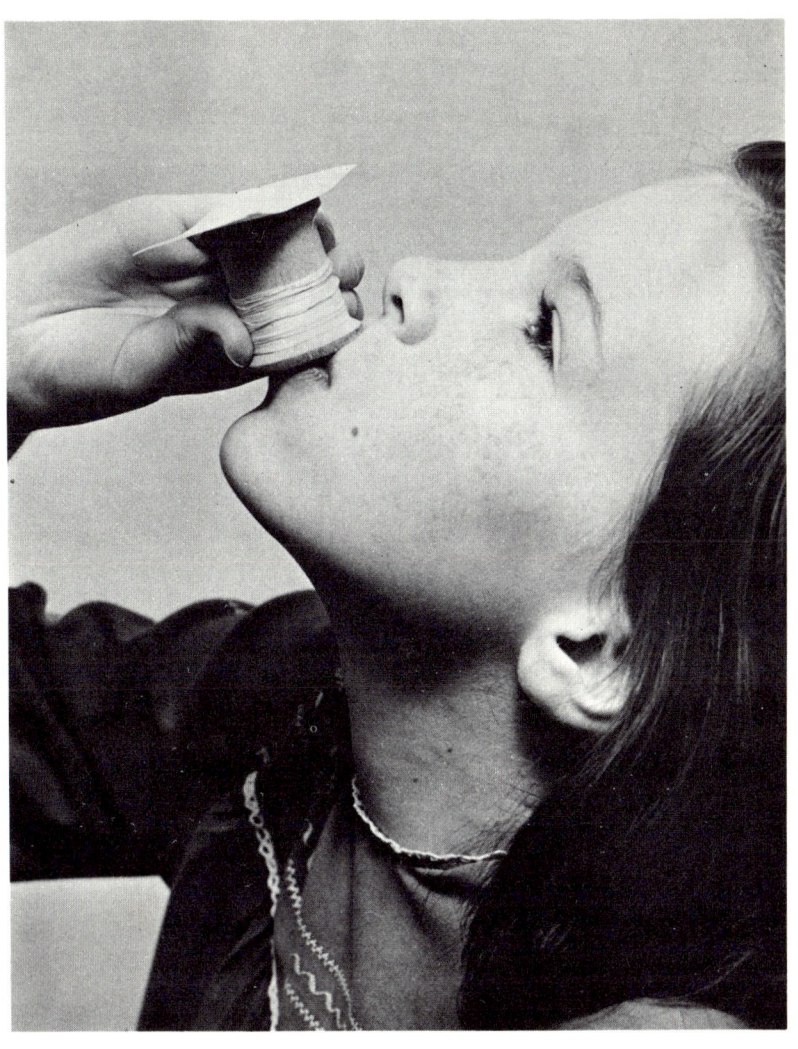

A variation is shown here. Attach a funnel to the hose of a vacuum cleaner. Put the hose in the back of the cleaner so that air blows *out*. If the funnel is held downward over a table tennis ball the air will pick up the ball, even though it is blowing outward from the funnel. Lift the hose slowly, and the ball sticks in the bottom of it. If the hose is held up, as in the top drawing, and the ball placed as shown, the air will support it.

In the upper drawing the air pressure keeps the ball up. It stays about in the center of the air stream, since if it falls slightly to the side, the more rapidly moving air toward the center exerts less pressure, and the more slowly moving air moves the ball back toward the center.

In the center drawing (B) the more slowly moving air on the top of the ball exerts more pressure than the rapidly moving air coming out of the funnel around the sides of the ball.

The same applies to the drawing (C). The slowly moving or still air behind the ball lifts it up into the funnel.

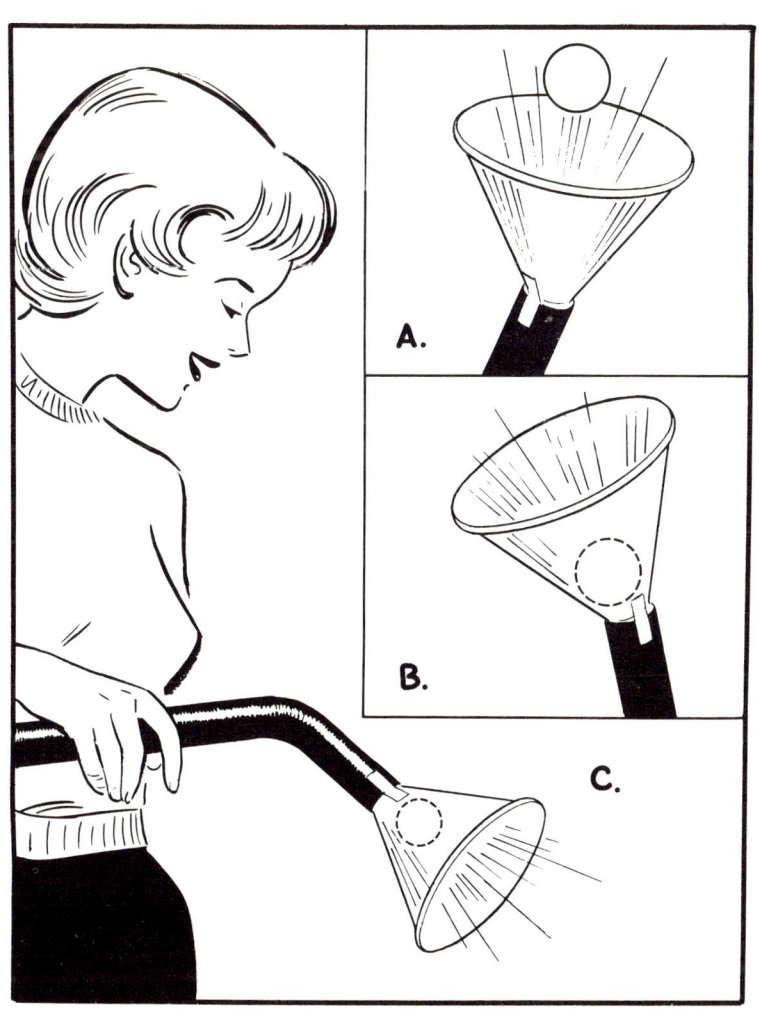

A water stream coming from a hose can be used to show the Bernoulli principle. The table tennis ball will stay at the top of the water stream.

# Benjamin Franklin
## 1706-1790

"Benjamin Franklin invented electricity" is a statement frequently heard. It is decidedly not true, of course.

But true indeed is the statement almost never heard, that Franklin invented the principle on which our present-day electrostatic copying machines operate.

Amazing is the scientific accomplishment of this man who devoted most of his life to other fields. He did not invent electricity, but he certainly was one of the first electrical pioneers.

A lengthy biography of Franklin is not necessary here. Every schoolchild knows about the boy, born in Boston, who ran away to Philadelphia to seek his fortune and walked up Market Street with loaves of bread under his arms, eating contentedly.

His writings added to our knowledge of geology, meteorology, seismology, physics, chemistry, astronomy, agriculture, history, printing, writing, philosophy, mathematics, hydrography, aeronautics, navigation, ethnology, botany, paleontology, medicine, and hygiene.

He is credited with being the first to use such words in electricity as armature, battery, brush, charged, charging, condense, conductor, discharge, electrical fire, electrical shock, minus, plus, negative, positive, electrician, electrified, Leyden bottle, nonconducting, nonelectric, stroke, uncharged.

His interest in electricity began when he saw some demonstrations by "a Doctor Spence" who arrived from Scotland. This was in 1746. He devoted the next six years of his life mainly to this study, and in that period accomplished most of his discoveries.

"Electric fluid" was a common term for electricity in that day. Franklin was the first to note that there are two kinds, negative and positive. The Leyden jar was the only receptacle in which electricity could be stored. Franklin found that he could use flat plates or panes of glass, and so is the inventor of our present-day condensers or capacitors.

He was a keen observer; like many others, he was interested in knowing whether electricity and lightning were the same. In 1749 he wrote down the ways in which he found the two alike:

1. Both give light.
2. Both give the same color of light.
3. Lightning and electric sparks both take a crooked path.
4. Both are swift in motion.
5. Both are conducted by metals.
6. Both make a crack or noise.
7. Both subsist in water or ice.
8. Both rend bodies as they pass through.

9. Both destroy animals.
10. Both melt metals.
11. Both set fire to inflammable substances.
12. Both have a "sulphureous" smell.

He observed that electricity is attracted by points or flows easily from points, and wondered if it were not reasonable to believe that lightning, too, would act the same. This led to the invention of the lightning rod in 1752. His most famous experiment was with a kite, yet the date is unknown.

Franklin did *not* have a bolt of lightning flow down the kite string to his hand; he might not have lived if this had happened. One of his contemporaries, G. W. Richmann, the Swedish physicist, trying the same experiment with a metal rod instead of a kite, was killed in St. Petersburg in July, 1753.

This was supposedly a year after Franklin's kite flew. As he set out to fly his kite, Franklin told only his son of his intentions. He feared ridicule. The two went into a field at the approach of a thunderstorm, and sent the kite aloft near a shed where they could take shelter from the rain. The kite was made of two light strips of cedar, formed into a cross. A large silk handkerchief was stretched over them. Silk was chosen rather than paper, because the rain and wind would not be so likely to shred it. A sharp-pointed wire was attached to the upper end of the upright stick. This, Franklin thought, would attract the atmospheric electricity and allow it to flow down the hemp twine. An iron key and a silk ribbon were tied to the bottom of the twine. The key hung down, and the silk ribbon made an insulated handle by which the twine could be held.

Father and son waited until one cloud passed over. Nothing happened. But soon they saw that some of the loose threads on the hemp twine were standing out, charged with the electric fire. Franklin then brought his knuckle close to the key, and drew sparks.

This was proof that lightning and electricity are the same. Franklin was unaware that a somewhat similar experiment had been performed earlier by Frenchmen under direction of a scientist, Thomas-François D'Alibard. They did not use a kite, but a metal rod forty feet high. No boy or girl should ever try this experiment with either a kite or a rod. Franklin probably never would have tried it had he realized the danger. He got through with this experiment unhurt, and was almost killed with what we would consider a much tamer one.

On that occasion he was about to electrocute a turkey. He had connected several capacitors or condensers together, and accidentally let the charge from them pass through his body. He was knocked unconscious, and as he regained his senses he said, "Well, I meant to kill a turkey, and instead I nearly killed a goose."

Two of his inventions, the improved heating stove, called the Franklin stove, and the lightning rod, could have made him rich, but he preferred not to patent his inventions. He wanted to give them to humanity.

The lightning rod brought criticism from some religious persons who believed that man should not meddle in the affairs of God. Thunder and lightning were considered by some to be expressions of wrath from the Almighty. Franklin, perhaps in an attempt to pacify his critics, wrote in *Poor Richard*:

"It has pleased God in His goodness to mankind, at length to discover to them the means of securing their habitations and other buildings from mischief by thunder and lightning."

Franklin did not invent the balloon, but when he saw the first successful one in Paris, in 1783, his was the classic reply to those who question the value of pure science and new inventions. "What good is it?" asked a bystander, as the balloon soared into the sky. "What good is a newborn baby?" Franklin replied.

He made many observations in physics and the other sciences, sound observations that he dutifully wrote about in letters, never in any formal scientific reports. One such observation concerned the conduction of heat.

He noticed that on a cold day the lock on his desk felt cold to his hand, although the wooden part of the desk, which must have been the same temperature, did not feel as cold. He concluded that the wood was not a good conductor of heat, whereas the metal was; which was why the wood did not conduct the heat away from his hand as rapidly as did the metal lock.

He was interested in music, as are most scientists, and was intrigued by the musical sounds produced on glasses of water when wet fingers were rubbed over their rims. Musicians play such glasses today, and there are even phonograph records of their music. Franklin invented an improvement. He built his glasses on a spindle, one glass overlapping the other, so that they turned by means of a foot pedal. The performer could touch their rims with the fingers of both hands and play four-part harmony. The instrument was called the "armonica." It was popular as a musical instrument for many years, and such composers as Beethoven, Gluck, and Mozart wrote music for it. It was sometimes called the "glass harmonica."

Franklin studied the flow of ocean currents, and was the first to chart the flow of the Gulf Stream.

He introduced the practice of applying lime to acid soils, although the farmers were slow to adopt his recommendations. He studied and reported on the difference in light absorption of various colors of cloth.

The bifocal lens for eyeglasses was Franklin's invention. This allows a person with changing vision to read clearly, then to see distant objects merely by raising his eyes. Franklin had been using two pairs of glasses; he simply combined them into one frame.

Franklin was among the first to understand some of the scientific aspects of weather forecasting. Because of a storm one night in 1743, he was unable to see an eclipse of the moon. Through newspapers he learned the path the storm had taken through a thousand miles of countryside, and this knowledge led to his investigation of the causes of storms.

That same year he proposed the formation of the American Philosophical Society and offered himself as its first secretary. The Royal Society awarded him the Sir Godfrey Copley gold medal on November 30, 1753, "on account of his curious experiments and observations on electricity." In May, 1756, he was elected a member of the Royal Society. Franklin wrote that he had never expected such an honor.

Most of his life Franklin spent in service to his country, as every school pupil knows. Only a very small part of his life was devoted to science. During his last years he expressed the hope that he might retire from public service, return to science, and resume his experiments. This hope was not realized. He died at the age of eighty-four.

Electrical experiments were parlor pastimes in Franklin's day. One of his favorites with which he entertained guests was the production of mysterious drawings on a piece of glass.

He would charge the glass before the guests saw it, by rubbing it, then would make the drawing with his finger. Of course, nothing showed on the glass until the moment of his trick. Before the guests he would sprinkle lycopodium powder on the glass, blow off the surplus, and the outline of the drawing would be seen.

The easy way to repeat this experiment (certainly not one of the best, but interesting) is to use an old phonograph record, charging it by brisk rubbing with a piece of wool. "Draw" on the record with a finger. The drawing is invisible.

Place flour on a cardboard, and blow it onto the record. The flour will be attracted to the record, but the attraction will be greater where the finger had not marked the figure or drawing, and the drawing will be seen, rather indistinctly.

This is the principle on which present-day electrostatic copying machines work. This and other experiments in static electricity work best when the humidity is low. They may not work at all in high humidity.

Franklin's experiment on light absorption by different colors of cloth is an easy one to do. The colors he used were black, deep blue, green, purple, red, yellow, white, and other shades. He laid them out on the snow, in bright sunlight.

In a few hours the black, which was warmed most by the absorption of light, had sunk deep into the snow. The dark blue had sunk almost as low, the lighter blue not quite so much, and the other colors less. The white had not sunk at all.

His practical conclusion was that soldiers and seamen who must march and work in the sun should wear white clothing in warm climates.

If no snow is at hand, the experiment may be performed on a cake of ice from the refrigerator. A strong light shining on it may be used if sunlight is not available.

The chance touching of the metal lock on his desk led Franklin into a study of heat conduction. He knew that the lock and the wood of the desk must be the same temperature, yet when he touched the metal lock it seemed much colder than the wood. He concluded that metal conducts heat much more readily than wood.

Franklin himself suggests an experiment to prove this:

"Take a piece of wood of the size and shape of a dollar between the thumb and fingers of one hand," he wrote, "and a dollar in like manner with the other hand; place the edges of both, at the same time, in the flame of a candle; and though the edge of the wooden piece takes flame and the metal piece does not, yet you will be obliged to drop the latter before the former, it conducting the heat more suddenly to your fingers."

He concluded that the reason woolen garments keep the body warmer than linen of the same thickness is that wool does not conduct the body heat to the outside air as readily as does the linen.

# Joseph Priestley
## 1733-1804

A brewery was an important factor in the life of a great chemist, Joseph Priestley. It led to the identification of carbon dioxide, the chief element of the carbonated soft-drink industry, and was a major cause of Priestley's decision to leave the ministry and devote his life to science.

Joseph was born in Leeds, England, the son of a poor weaver who died when the boy was seven years of age. He was taken by an aunt who was a member of a religious group called "Dissenters." She sent Joseph to an academy of her faith to study for the ministry.

He was a bright student, and learned quickly, but a speech impediment would have prevented him from ever becoming a pastor of a large church. He became pastor of a small one, and to make ends meet he taught school all day and then did private tutoring at night. He attended some lectures on chemistry and began to experiment.

Benjamin Franklin came to London, where the two met. Franklin was so impressed with the intelligent young man that he urged him to write a book about the history and development of electricity. It was so well received that he was invited to membership in the Royal Society in 1766.

Priestley lived next to a brewery, and was fascinated by the gas that came out of the vats. He got permission to study it. He saw that a flame would die out in it. There was another way of producing it, he found, by the action of sulphuric acid on chalk, and he learned how to dissolve it in water. This was the beginning of the soft-drink industry, but Priestley had no desire to make money out of it, even if he had known how.

The good church people could not understand a pastor who spent time in a brewery, and Priestley was equally ready to give up the church position and devote more time to his experiments. This became possible when Lord Shelburne, a scholar, employed him as his librarian, and with the job offered him a laboratory in which to work.

Priestley's greatest discovery, perhaps, was oxygen. He found that mercuric oxide, when heated, gave off four to five times its own volume of a gas, which caused a candle to "burn with splendor" and red-hot wood splinters to "sparkle." He also found that a mouse could live longer in a closed container filled with the new gas than in one of air only.

But also of magnitude was his discovery of the cycle of nature in which growing plants give off oxygen and absorb carbon dioxide. He wrote of this discovery, and is quoted in the *Scientific American* book *Lives in Science* as follows:

"I have been so happy as by accident to have hit upon a method of restoring air which has been injured by the burning of candles, and to have discovered at least one of the restoratives which Nature employs for this purpose. It is vegetation.

"On the 17th of August, 1771, I put a sprig of mint into a quantity of air which a wax candle had burned out, and found that on the 27th of the same month, another candle burned perfectly well in it. This experiment I repeated without the least variation in the event, not less than eight or 10 times in the remainder of the summer. . ."

Other gases isolated by Priestley included ammonia, nitrogen, nitric oxide, carbon monoxide, and sulphur dioxide. Still, he found time to write on education and ethics.

He sympathized with the American colonists in their struggle for independence. He advocated the separation of church and state. On Bastille day, in 1791, he celebrated the event in Birmingham with a group of friends, and this infuriated a mob. The mob burned his house and laboratory, scattered his valuable papers, and drove the family off to London. They lived there the next two years, then sailed to America, where they were received as great friends and celebrities.

Priestley was received by George Washington and Franklin, and became a close friend to Thomas Jefferson. He settled in Northumberland, Pennsylvania, where his two sons had settled two years earlier. There he set up his laboratory and continued his experiments. He died in 1854, at seventy years of age. His home in Northumberland is a museum, and some of his laboratory equipment may still be seen there.

To reproduce Priestley's experiment on the cycle of nature, get a large glass jar with a tight-fitting lid. A restaurant-type mayonnaise jar is good. Get a candle, tie a wire around it so that it can be let down into the jar, and dig some plants with dirt around their roots, to grow in the jar. The author found that clover dug from the edge of a flower bed worked very well.

Plant the greenery in the jar, put some water in the dirt, and light the candle. Lower the candle into the jar, then close the lid. As the oxygen is used up, the candle grows dimmer, and goes out entirely.

Leave the candle in the jar, with the lid closed tightly. In twelve to twenty-four hours, take the candle out very carefully, to avoid letting air get into the jar. Light it, lower it again into the jar, and it should go out immediately, showing that there is very little or no oxygen in the jar.

Repeat: keep the jar closed this time for ten days. Keep it in the light, so that sunlight will let the plants grow. At the end of ten days, the candle will be seen to burn as long as it did the first time. This shows that the green leaves have absorbed the carbon dioxide and given off oxygen.

This was how Priestley discovered that the atmosphere of the world is "renewed" by green leaves. The experiment was performed in 1771.

# Alessandro Volta
## 1745-1827

Alessandro Volta was important as the man who discovered that the electricity that could make a frog's legs jerk did not come from the animal, as Luigi Galvani (1737–1798) believed, but from an external source. He was the inventor of the battery. We honor him every time we use the word "volt."

As a child, Alessandro was so quiet that his parents and neighbors in Como, Italy, thought he was not bright, but at school he learned rapidly; he soon proved to be very keen.

He liked chemistry and physics the moment he was introduced to those subjects. At seventeen he wrote a paper on electricity, and not long after he designed an electrophorus, an instrument for the production of electric charges by induction. The design has changed little in all the years that have passed. Students still make them very much like the one Volta made and used.

At twenty-nine Volta taught physics in the Como high school. In 1779 he became professor of physics at the University of Pavia, a chair he occupied for almost forty years. He was elected a Fellow of the Royal Society in England after his invention of a new electroscope, an instrument so sensitive that it could detect electric charges in water vapor and in smoke.

Galvani published a paper in 1791 in which he told of his experiments in "animal electricity." It told how he had caused animal muscles to move by means of electricity administered in several ways. Many other scientists began to repeat the experiments, checking Galvani's conclusions, as scientists always do when one of them delves into new ideas and explores new frontiers.

Galvani found that a muscle would move when a copper wire and a zinc wire were attached to it and then touched together. The copper he touched to the nerve, the zinc to the muscle. He concluded that the electricity to move the muscle was produced in the tissues themselves.

Volta began to doubt this, and began experiments to determine just where the current came from. He found that the muscle did not have to be part of the circuit, and by holding the two metals together and touching them to his tongue he could "taste" the electricity produced there. His experiments led to the invention of the "voltaic pile" and "crown of cups." These were the first batteries, and the batteries that power our transistor radios and flashlights owe their existence to these inventions.

The voltaic pile is described elsewhere (page 91).

The crown of cups was a series of cups containing salt water. Each cup contained a strip of silver and a strip of zinc, with the silver in one cup connected to the zinc in the next. Current was drawn from the last strips of silver and zinc.

When Volta published the results of his experiments he was awarded a high honor in science: the Copley Medal of the Royal Society.

He began to wish for a quiet life. In 1804 he asked to be allowed to resign his professorship at the University. One of his ardent admirers was Napoleon, who had made him a count in 1801. Napoleon persuaded Volta to remain at his post until 1818, when he retired to his native Como, to years of peace and happiness. He died at the age of eighty-two. It was in 1881 that the International Electrical Congress named the unit of electromotive force, "volt," in his honor.

Volta found that by touching the ends of a copper and a zinc wire together and touching the other ends to his tongue, he could "taste" the electricity produced. This experiment can be repeated by using a silver dime and a copper cent. Touch them together and at the same time touch them to the tongue. A piece of aluminum foil used in place of the copper coin will give a sharper taste.

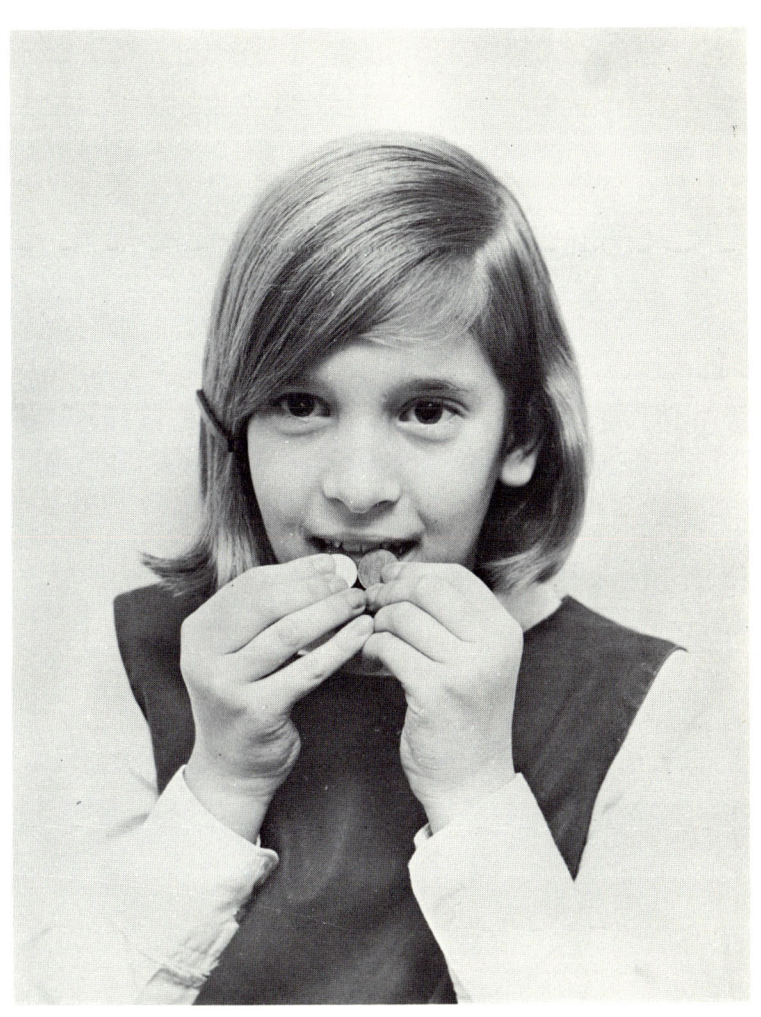

The electrophorus works only when the air is dry. Winter, on a cold day in a warm house, is the best time. Place an old phonograph record on a table and rub it ten seconds or more with wool. Note that the girl is holding an aluminum pie tin by criss-crossed nylon threads.

Place the tin on the record and touch it with the finger to discharge the top side. Look carefully; a spark is seen as the finger is approached. Lift the tin by the threads, and another spark can be drawn from it—to the knuckle or to the nose!

Volta invented the electrophorus in 1775. He found that he could charge a plate of rosin or hard rubber by rubbing it, place an insulated metal disk on it, discharge the disk with a finger, remove the disk, then get a considerable spark from it.

It is simple to duplicate Volta's experiment with objects found around the house. Place an old long-playing phonograph record on the table, rub it briskly for fifteen seconds with a woolen cloth or sweater. Place a metal plate on it, touch the plate to discharge it. Then lift the plate with an insulated handle or with silk or nylon threads tied to it. It will thus be charged so that a spark may be drawn from it to a person or metallic object.

Volta explained the operation as follows: Rubbing the rosin or record gives its upper surface a negative charge. The metal plate placed on it takes on a positive charge on its under surface and a negative charge on its upper surface. Touching the plate draws off the negative charge from the top, but the positive charge remains bound to the metal as long as it rests on the record. When it is removed, the positive charge is freed so that it may jump to another object. The metal plate may be charged and discharged several times without rubbing the record again; the action will continue until the charge on the record leaks into the air.

Any of several objects can be used as the metal plate: a toy saucepan from the toy counter, an aluminum pie pan with a plastic cover and handle, and a disposable aluminum pie tin with nylon threads for a handle.

Alessandro Volta's experiment in which he produced an electric battery may be repeated easily. Get about fifty dimes (old silver dimes only), some aluminum foil, and paper towels from the kitchen, a frame to hold the stacked coins, and some strong salt water.

In the photo two frames are used, so that the coins will not be piled too high. The piles are connected by a wire.

Cut the foil and paper disks the size of the dimes. Blotting paper may be used instead of paper towels, and it will be found to handle better. Do not use blotters with a glossy side.

Dip the paper disks into the salt water, then take them out on the hand so that some of the water will drain off. They should not be dripping wet when placed on the coins.

Make the pile by alternately stacking first a dime, then a paper, then foil. Do not put paper on the foil, but make the pile as stated: dime, paper, foil, dime, paper, foil, etc.

When twenty-five to fifty of the dimes have been used in this way, wet the tips of the fingers in the solution, and touch the top and bottom of the pile with two fingers. A shock will be felt.

It is well to rub the wooden uprights in the frame with paraffin before the experiment begins, so the solution will run off and not soak into the wood to form a short circuit.

Strong ammonium chloride solution will give a stronger battery with fewer coins, but the solution of common salt and water will give plenty of shock. The shock will be harmless.

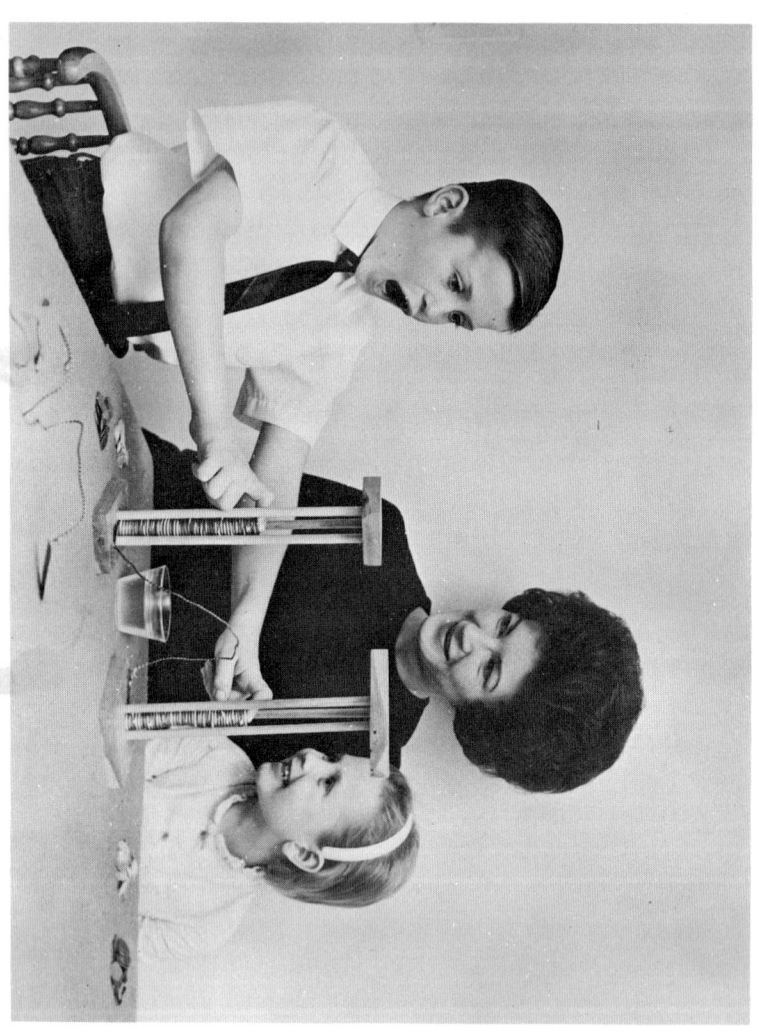

# William Henry
## 1774-1836

When we hear the term "Henry's law" we may be inclined to think of the great American scientist, Joseph Henry. But the law was named for another brilliant scientist, less known: William Henry of England.

William was born in Manchester, and educated at the Manchester Academy and the University of Edinburgh. He worked with his father, assisting him in his medical practice, then returned to the University, where he took his M.D. degree in 1807.

Before this, however, he did intensive studies in chemistry, and wrote several important papers which were read to the Royal Society. In one of his writings he described his findings in regard to the quantity of gases absorbed in water at different pressures and at different temperatures. From this came the term "Henry's law."

William Henry was an attractive man, refined in

manner and eloquent in his speech. He was popular, both as a person and as a physician. A son, William Charles Henry, M.D., wrote the biographical notices that are found in a few books.

It is interesting that, while he was a Fellow of the Royal Society, known for his work in science, he was also interested in the humanities and wrote several literary essays, among them "Cursory Remarks on Music." It is not unusual for a scientist to be interested in music.

Henry's law states that the solubility of gases in liquids is directly proportional to the pressure of the gas above the liquid, if the temperature remains constant.

This may be seen when a bottle of soft drink is opened. As the pressure is released when the cap is removed, some of the gas bubbles out of the liquid. This is the simplest demonstration, but not the most accurate, since the carbon dioxide in the soft drink not only dissolves in the water but forms a few unstable compounds with it.

Henry's law in regard to temperature may be observed when tap water is heated. The warmer the water, the less gas it will hold, so that as the water is heated, bubbles of gas are seen to come out of it, many of them lodging at the sides of the container.

Carbon dioxide, dissolved under pressure in the liquid, does not bubble or foam until the cap is removed, reducing the pressure on the surface of the liquid.

When the pressure is reduced the liquid cannot hold as much of the gas, and so some of it is released from solution in the form of bubbles.

## René Théophile Hyacinthe Laënnec
## 1781-1826

One day some children, observed by an alert young doctor, made an experiment that resulted in the invention of the stethoscope—one of the most important instruments of medicine.

The children were at a seesaw, but they were not riding up and down. While one held his ear to one end of the board, the other would scratch the opposite end with a pin. They were marveling at the way sound traveled through the wood.

The young doctor, René Laënnec, watched and remembered. In later years, his bashfulness caused him to recall the incident.

Laënnec was born in the French province of Brittany. His mother died when he was five and he was sent to live with an uncle, a priest. Later he was sent to another uncle, a physician in Nantes. This uncle was to be a real influence in the boy's life. In 1795 René started his studies in medicine at Nantes and was a brilliant student. He served with the republican armies as an assistant surgeon and later went to Paris as the pupil of Napoleon's physician, Jean Nicolas Corvisart, the well-known professor of medicine.

He was disappointed at not being appointed to practice in a hospital, but soon built up a good medical practice. He became editor of the *Journal of Medicine*. He was finally appointed to a hospital in 1816, and it was there he invented the stethoscope.

According to his own account, he was called in 1816 to diagnose the illness of a young girl who was abnormally fat. He knew that he could not hear much by putting his ear to her chest, as was the custom of doctors of the time, and besides, he was too timid to listen to her heart and chest in that manner.

He remembered the children he had watched as they listened to the scratching of the pin heard through the wooden plank. He took what he called a "sheaf" of paper, rolled it up tight, placed one end of it against the girl's chest and put his ear to the other end. He was "both surprised and gratified," he wrote, at being able to hear the heart sounds more distinctly than he had ever heard them when putting his ear directly to a patient's chest.

He improved this device by making a wooden tube. A small hole went through the length of the tube, with one end hollowed out. When the hollowed-out end was placed against the chest and the small hole in the other end placed at his ear, the heartbeat was far more audible. This is the principle of the modern stethoscope. He himself never used the term "stethoscope." He always referred to it as a "baton."

Laënnec also developed a new method of diagnosing diseases of the heart and lungs—by listening.

He wrote a book on the subject, and was immediately attacked by physicians who did not agree with him. Joseph Victor Broussais, leader of the opposition, believed that all vital processes were brought about by "irritation," that all disease was caused by too much or not enough "irritation."

It was the custom of physicians of the day to bleed their patients to "get rid of the bad blood." Many patients actually died from loss of blood—a whole quart was taken from President George Washington, and this may have hastened his death. Laënnec opposed the practice, which brought him much criticism and ridicule. It was not the practice which brought the ridicule, it was Laënnec's opposition to it.

His health was never good. He contracted tuberculosis, one of the diseases he had taught doctors to diagnose correctly. He died at the age of forty-five.

Place one end of a plank at the ear, scratch the other end; the sound traveling through the wood may be heard distinctly. This was an experiment performed by children at a seesaw, which led Laënnec to the invention of the stethoscope.

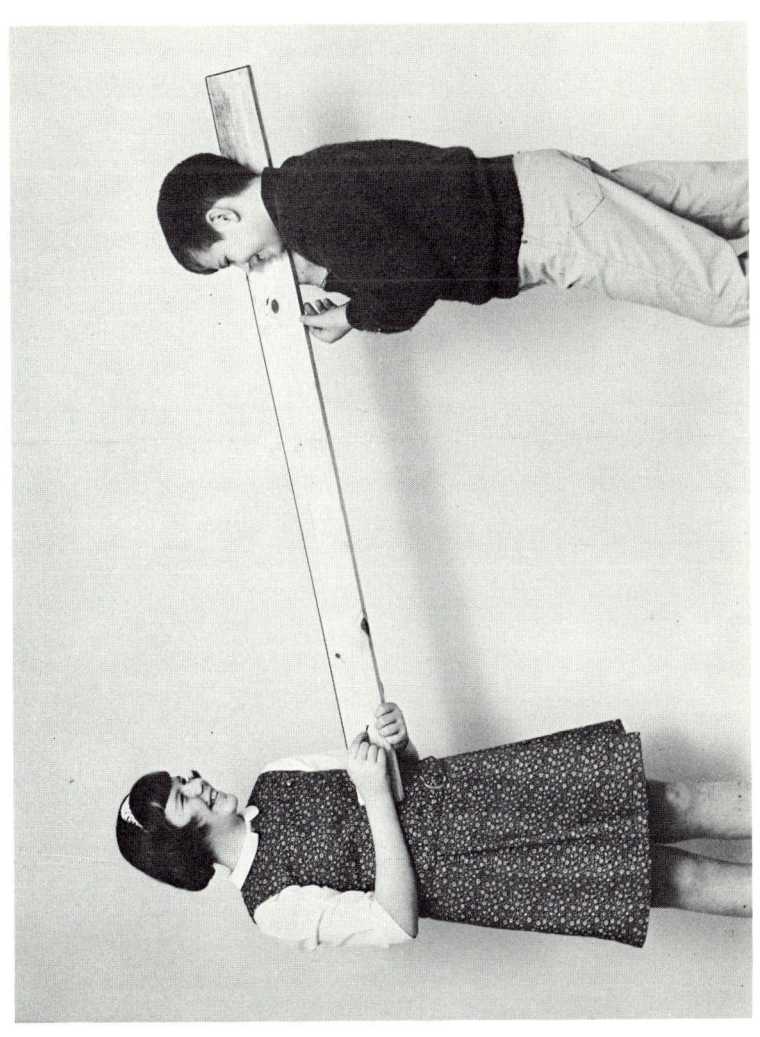

Laënnec's first stethoscope was a roll of paper, by which he listened to the sounds in a patient's chest.

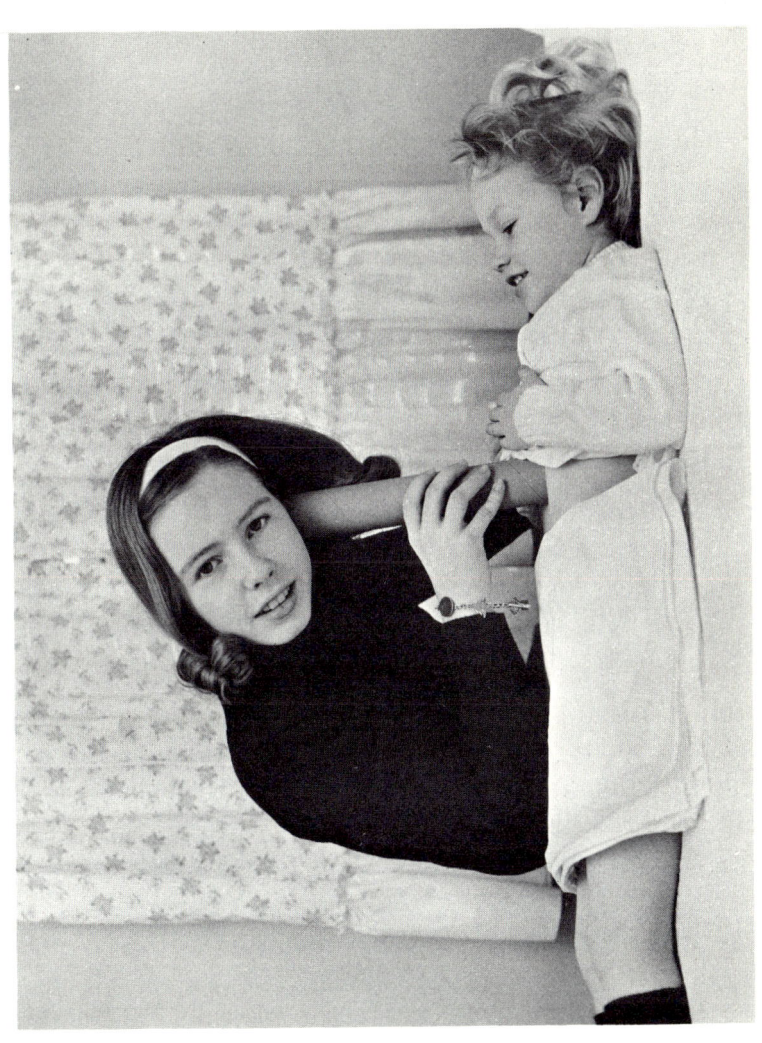

The surprising ease with which sound travels through a tube can be shown with a long cardboard tube. The one shown is more than five feet long.

The boy could not hear the ticking of the girl's wrist watch at that distance without the tube. But when she held the watch at one end of the tube and the boy held his ear to the other end the ticks could be distinctly heard.

Sound waves normally spread out in circles from the sound source, getting weaker as the circles get larger. The tube confines some of the waves so they do not spread out, and they travel along inside the tube without diminishing so much in loudness.

An experimental stethoscope can be made with a funnel and a rubber tube. The stethoscopes used by doctors today are refinements of this crude instrument. To make the stethoscope, put the hose on the funnel, hold the other end of the hose to the ear, and place the funnel against the bare chest (page 106).

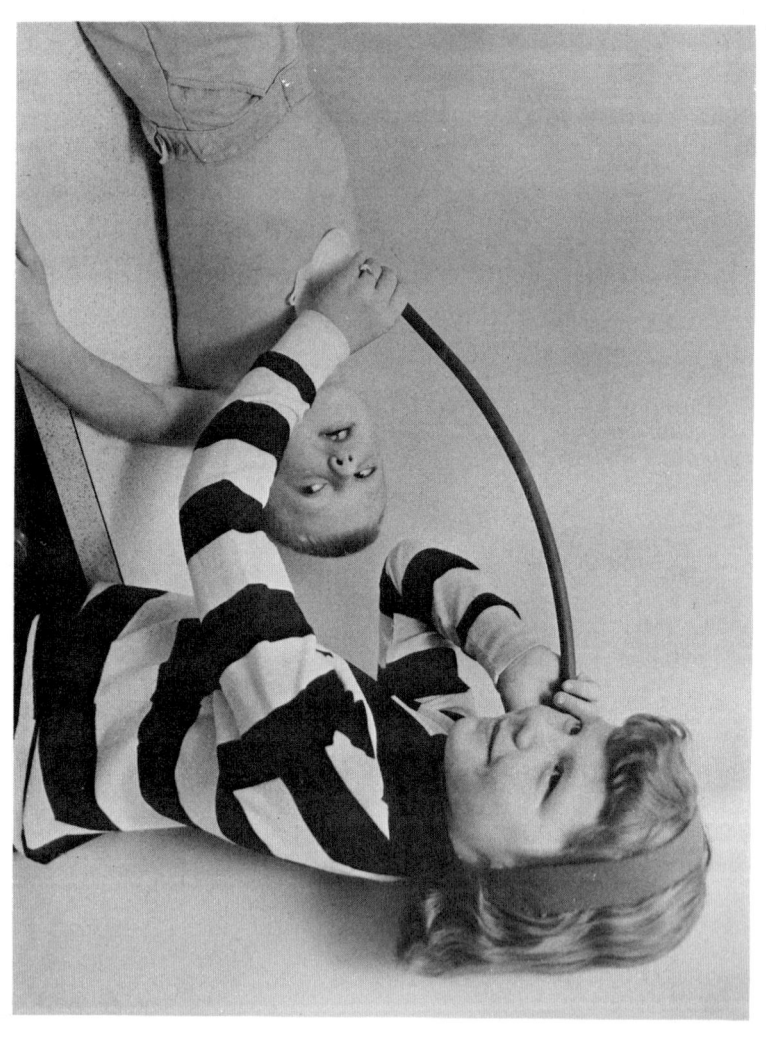

# Michael Faraday
## 1791-1867

Michael Faraday moved a bar magnet inside a wire coil and made a little compass needle wiggle. The wiggle meant to him that the moving magnet had caused an electric current to flow in the wire. He had discovered the answer to a problem that had perplexed great minds. It had a great meaning for civilization—all of our large electric generating plants operate on the principle revealed by that little wiggling needle.

Many scientists had seen the magnet needle move because of electric current flowing through a wire, and had believed that, if the current could move a magnet, a magnet should in some way be made to produce a current. They tried many arrangements of magnets, some of them quite fantastic, but to no avail. They had all missed the important secret: the magnet, to produce electricity in a wire, must *move*.

Michael was born in London, the son of a blacksmith father and a mother who could barely read and write. The family was very poor and lived in small quarters above a coach house, where neither the odors nor the associations of the district could have been inspiring to a young boy.

Michael was nine when his father died. A year later he served as errand boy with a stationer and bookseller near his home. He was a good worker, and in 1805 became an apprentice bookbinder in the bookshop. He was introduced to the wonderful world of science upon reading *Mrs. Marcet's Conversations on Chemistry*.

He had a chance to read many of the books on which he worked, and others besides, including the encyclopedia. He became more and more interested in science, electricity in particular. He attended lectures by prominent scientists, including Sir Humphry Davy.

He scraped together the materials for simple experiments, and in a letter to a friend, in 1812, he describes his experience with a Voltaic pile, giving us a glimpse of the young man's enthusiasm and sense of humor.

"I, Sir, I my own self," he wrote, "cut out seven discs of the size of halfpennies each! I, Sir, covered them with seven halfpence, and I interposed between seven, or rather six, pieces of paper soaked in a solution of muriate of soda! But laugh no longer, Dear A.; rather wonder at the effects this trivial power produced. It was sufficient to produce the decomposition of sulphate of magnesia—an effect which extremely surprised me; for I did not, could not, have any idea that the agent was competent to the purpose."

He made notes at a Davy lecture, and as his apprenticeship came to an end, he sent them, with a letter of application, to the great Davy. The notes were handsomely bound in a volume, the title page and subtitles equisitely pen-printed in decorative lettering. He got the job—how could Davy refuse, when such a compliment was paid to him?

Faraday at the age of twenty-one became an assistant in the laboratory of the Royal Institution, working with Davy. There was not much money, but the youth was happy to get out of the bookbinder trade and to work in science.

He had long believed that, since an electric current turns a bar of iron into a magnet, a magnet should in some way produce an electric current. He never lost sight of this belief, although he, alone or with Davy, worked long on these experiments and investigations. In 1831, he solved the problem.

He discovered that the magnet will produce the current, but to do so the magnet must be *in motion*. If the magnet is thrust into a coil a current is produced; when it is pulled out, another current, in the opposite direction, is produced. He also discovered that an uneven current in one wire can induce a current in a parallel wire, without any connection between the two. These discoveries led to the dynamo and the transformer—machines that make possible the production and handling and transmission of the tremendous quantities of electric power used today.

These were Faraday's greatest discoveries, but others followed. He learned to liquefy a number of gases. He learned to form several original chemical compounds. He worked on crystals, oils, lenses, ventilation problems, and fog signals—and accomplished good results in these fields.

In other fields he was not so successful; for example, he worked on the theory of the connection between gravity and electricity—a problem which today is still unsolved.

Many honors came to him. The Rumford and Royal medals were conferred on him in 1846. In his latter years, as his memory began to fail, Prince Albert and the Queen gave him a house on Hampton Court Green, where he lived with his wife and niece until his death.

Davy and Faraday had their disagreements, and there was some rancor at one time. Still, when a newspaper reporter asked Davy, old, blind, and almost near the end of his life, what his greatest discovery was, he replied without hesitation, "Michael Faraday!"

There are two easy ways to make a galvanometer. One is to wind insulated wire around a compass. One or two turns will measure rather small currents of electricity by making the compass needle turn at right angles to the turns of wire. More turns make the instrument more sensitive. The wire will stay on the compass better if a piece of cardboard is placed around it, as in the second drawing.

Another easy way is to wind wire around a matchbox in which a magnetized needle is suspended. The needle may be suspended by a small thread and a small piece of cardboard. The closer the turns of wire are to the needle the more sensitive it is. At $A$ the complete instrument is seen; at $B$ a cross section showing the needle and the turns of wire above and below it.

Connect the ends of an insulated wire wound several times around a tube to the galvanometer just made. Push the magnet in and out of the tube, and the galvanometer needle will be seen to move with each push. This is the experiment Faraday made, showing that magnetism can produce electricity. It is the basic principle of our present-day electric generating plants.

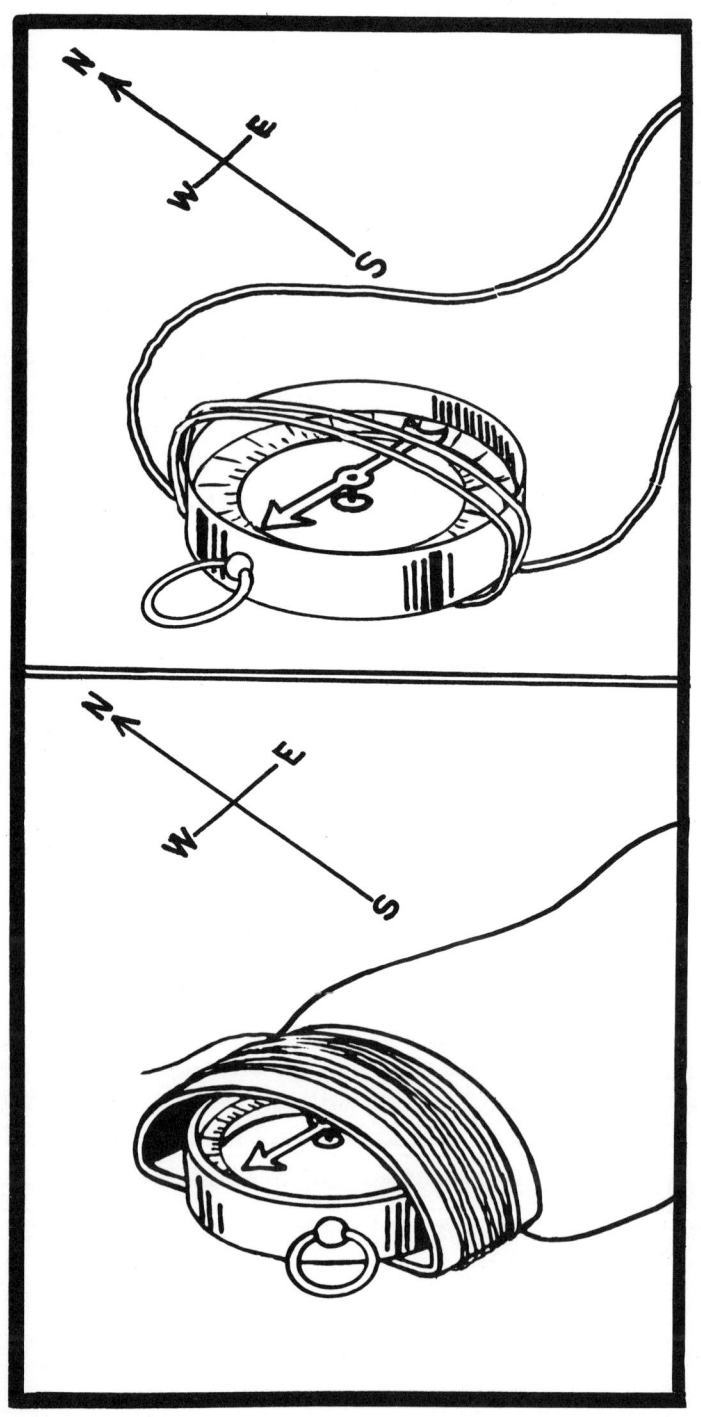

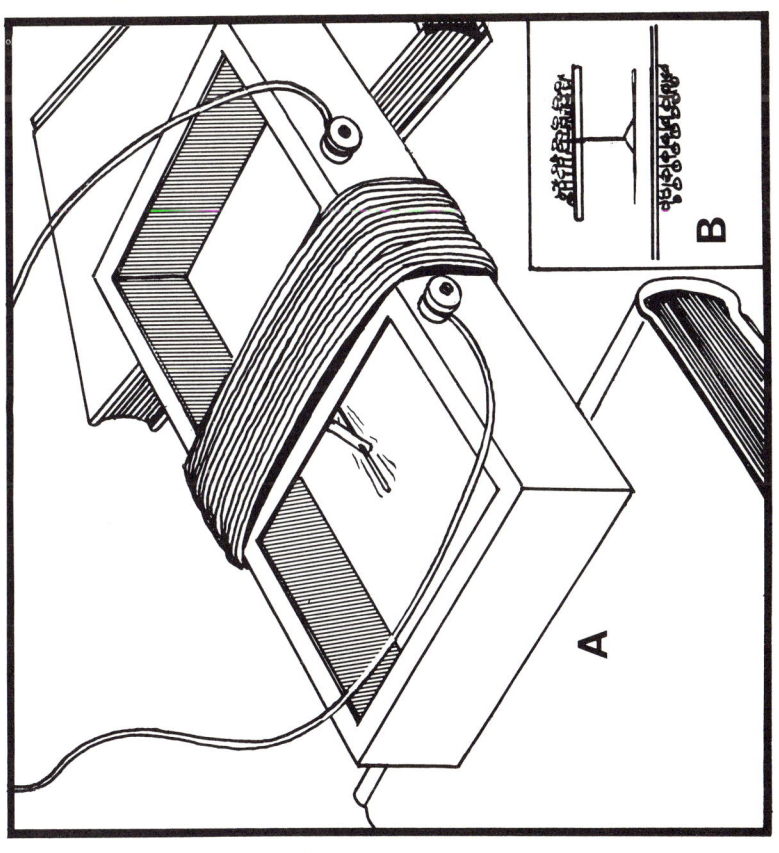

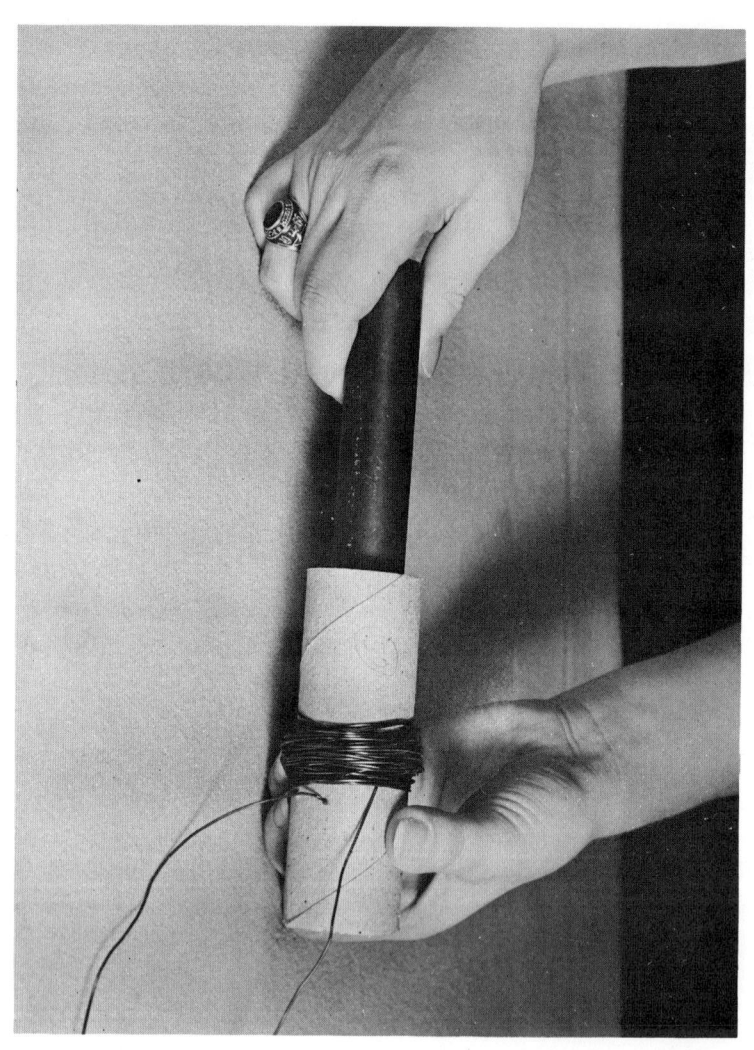

# Joseph Henry
## 1799-1878

Joseph Henry's chance reading of a science book is credited with starting him on the path to become a great American scientist. Perhaps, too, the family's poverty helped make him a great man.

He was born in Albany, New York, but the date of his birth is not definitely known. It is thought to be 1799. When Joseph was six his parents sent him to live with relatives in Galway, thirty-six miles away.

The parents thought this necessary, in order that the boy might be better fed and allow his mother to devote more time to the care of his ailing father.

Joseph attended the village school and at ten was given a morning job in the village store. The proprietor sent the boy to afternoon classes in school and encouraged him to seek a good education. Joseph's problems included an inability to make decisions; later in his life he told a story about himself to illustrate the comedy of his indecisions and hesitations.

He could not make up his mind whether he wanted square or round toes on the new shoes he had ordered. He made several trips to the cobbler's shop, and kept putting off the decision. On one of the trips he was surprised to find the shoes finished, one toe round and the other square.

One day he discovered that he could slip into the church library by crawling under the church floor. Thus he began to read books he found there. His employer discovered the method of Joseph's entry into the little room, and arranged for him to enter by the door. As Joseph read the books, he and his kindly employer discussed them.

At fourteen his father died, and Joseph returned to his mother in Albany. The mother apprenticed him to a watchmaker and silversmith. The work did not interest him, although he did acquire some skill in the use of his hands. He became interested in the theater, and began to work backstage, writing plays and acting. He learned stage mannerisms that proved useful to him later when he was a professor and one of the best of all science demonstrators.

His mother took in boarders. One of them lent the boy Gregory's *Lectures on Experimental Philosophy, Astronomy, and Chemistry,* published in London in 1808. Joseph was captivated by the book. By the time he had read it through he was determined to make science his career. The stage was forgotten.

He started evening classes at Albany Academy, and in seven months qualified as a country schoolteacher. As he taught he continued his own studies in the evenings. An opening in the chemistry department in the academy developed, and he was given the job. Here he had access to laboratory equipment and set up the demonstrations which he used during his lectures. It was a time when engineers were in great demand. Henry gave up his job in Albany to work on the Erie Canal as a surveying engineer.

In 1862 he returned to teaching as a professor of science and mathematics at Albany Academy. Here, in the summers when the students were gone, he had opportunities to conduct his experiments.

William Sturgeon had invented the electromagnet in England. Henry improved it by wrapping the wire with silk for insulation, enabling him to wind the wire in several layers, adding greatly to the power of the magnet. He wound insulated wire around a soft iron bar, connecting the ends to a galvanometer. He placed the bar across the poles of his electromagnet. Thus he found that when the current was turned on in the wires leading to his magnet, the galvanometer needle turned slightly; and again when the current was turned off, the needle turned slightly in the opposite direction.

He had discovered the principle of the transformer, or of electromagnetic induction. But ask someone, and the answer is likely to be that the discoverer of this important phenomenon was Faraday. Both men were working on the problem, Faraday in London, and Henry in Albany. Henry failed to publish his findings, so Faraday received the credit.

When Henry did get around to publishing his findings, however, they won him an appointment to the faculty of Princeton University, where he taught and did research. He remained there from 1832 to 1846.

Henry invented the telegraph, and had one working over a distance of a mile before Samuel F. B. Morse, who received the credit, entered the picture. Henry invented the telegraph relay, which is still used in modified form in almost all electric equipment today.

In 1842 Henry demonstrated the transmission of radio waves. He set up his spark gap in his laboratory, and thirty feet away picked up energy in a coil of wire to deflect a needle. At that time the importance of this was not realized; fifty years went by before Hertz performed almost the same experiment—and received credit for discovering radio waves. Henry was the first to describe an electric motor. His motor had a part that moved up and down instead of a wheel that turned, but it was the beginning of the use of electricity for the production of movement.

Almost every application of electricity today uses one or more of the principles discovered by Henry. These include the transmission of power over long-distance lines, which depends upon transformers. Other men contributed to the developments, but Henry discovered the principles. The telephone is an example.

The Smithsonian Institution was founded in 1846, and Henry was appointed its executive head. He continued in this capacity until his death in 1878.

Many of the terms of electricity are well known—volts and amperes, for example. But an important term, less well known, is the henry—named for Joseph Henry—a measurement of inductance concerning magnetic fields in instruments and systems.

What is thought to be the first electric motor was announced by Henry in *Silliman's Journal*, July, 1831, in which he is quoted as saying:

"I have lately succeeded in producing motion in a little machine by a power which I believe has never been applied in mechanics, by magnetic attraction and repulsion.

"Not much importance, however, is attached to

the invention, since the article, in its present state, can only be considered a philosophical toy; although in the progress of discovery and invention, it is not impossible that the same principle, or some modification of it on a more extended scale, may hereafter be applied to some useful purpose."

We can make a model of Henry's motor, accurate except that he used mercury cups for making his contacts.

In the drawing, *A* is a wooden base. Four strips of galvanized metal, cut from a tin can, are represented by *B*. These are attached so that when the copper wires, *D*, strike them, they bend downward, only to spring upward again as the wires are raised again.

Two small permanent magnets are used, shown at *C*. *E* is the armature or rocking bar. It is made from a large nail or spike, with the point and head sawed off. It is wound with No. 20 bell wire, with the turns closely spaced. The author had enough to wind from one end of the bar to the other and halfway back again. The number of turns is not important.

The rocking bar is supported on a small nail extending through two wooden supports which are screwed to the base. *V* represents the wires that connect to a battery. A toy transformer will not work on this; direct current is required, and the polarity must be correct. If the machine does not work, reverse the wires *V* where they connect to the battery.

The photo shows the completed motor, as a boy touches the wire to a three-cell battery.

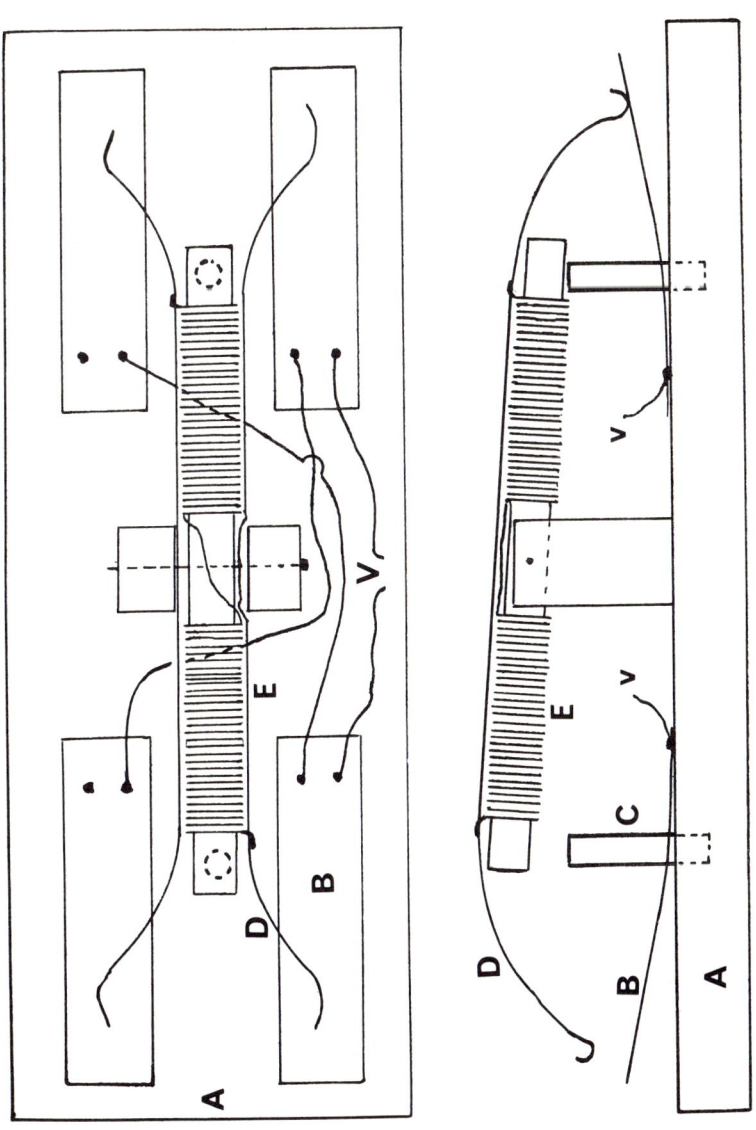

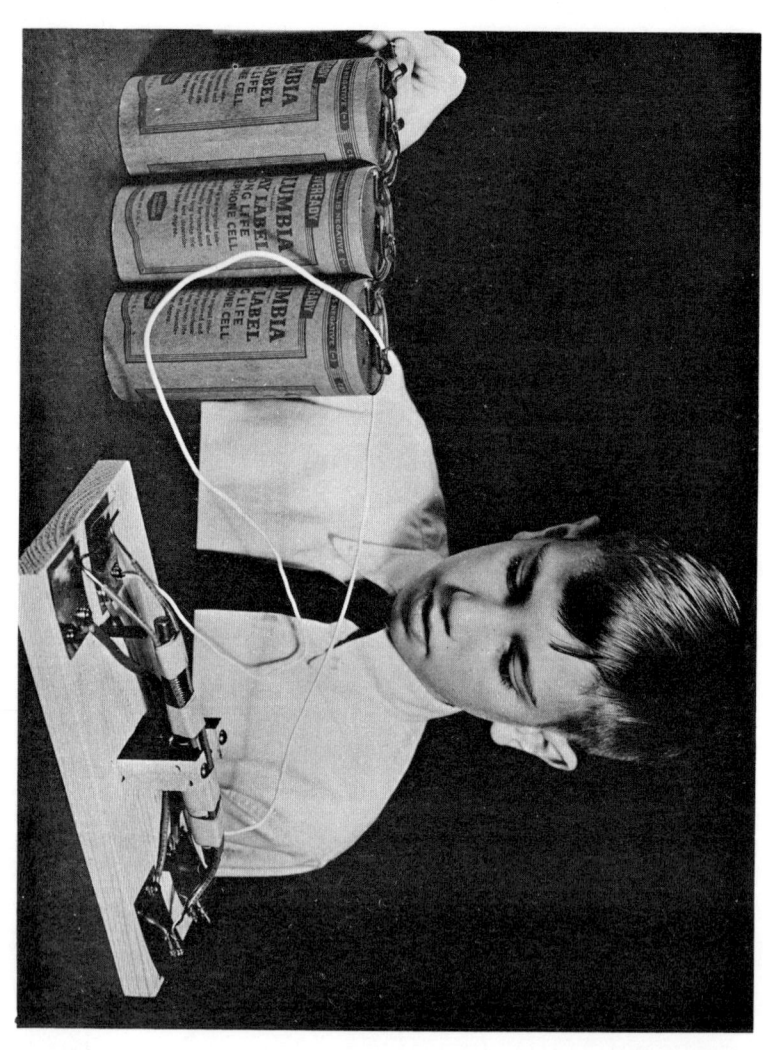

This is Henry's first crude transformer, the forerunner of millions of transformers used today in almost every electric device and circuit. The model is practically the same as Henry's—the main difference is that Henry used heavier iron.

In the diagram, $A$ is the source of current. This can be any battery or cell. In the photo, the girl is using a flashlight cell.

$B$ is the primary coil, wound on a U bolt, $C$. The author used 100 turns of bell wire to make the primary. $E$ is the secondary, wound on the strip of 3/16-inch iron. This strip comes with the U bolt from a hardware store. The author used 65 turns of wire here.

When the wire is touched to the battery, the needle in the compass, $F$, will move. Two turns of wire around the compass should be sufficient, or possibly even one.

Place the compass so that the hand or needle is parallel with the wire. The passage of current will deflect the needle so that it moves toward a position at right angles to the wire. In the drawing this movement is exaggerated; the needle is not likely to move so far toward the right-angle position.

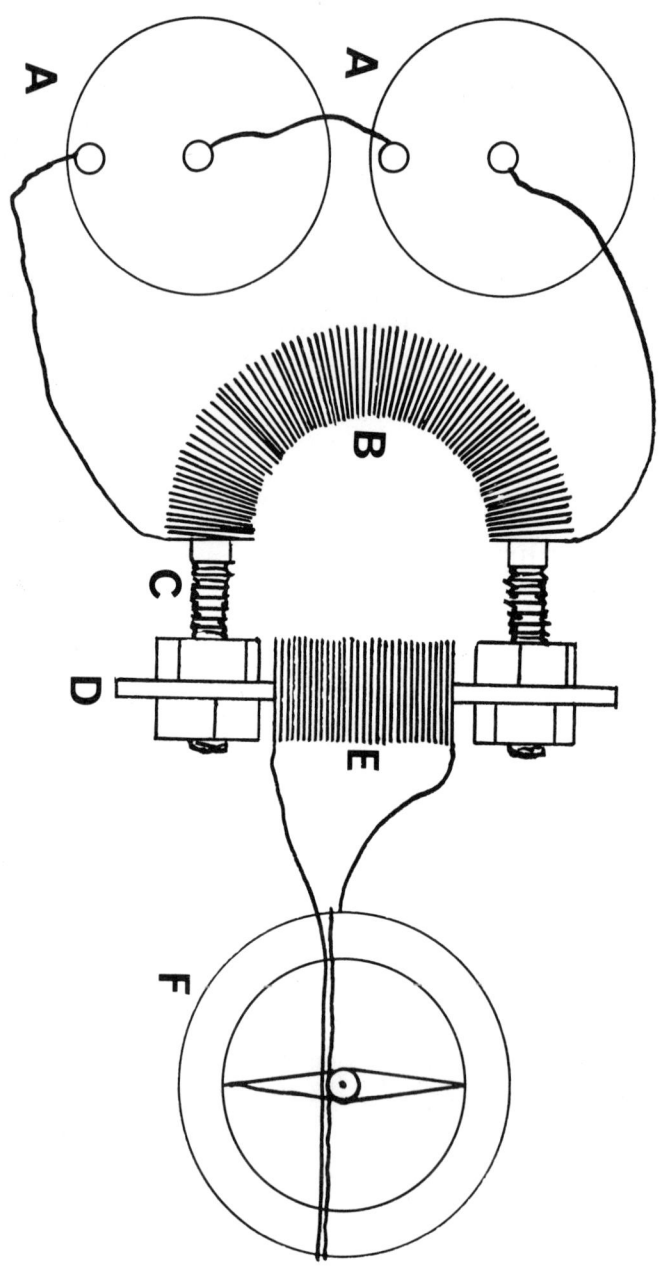

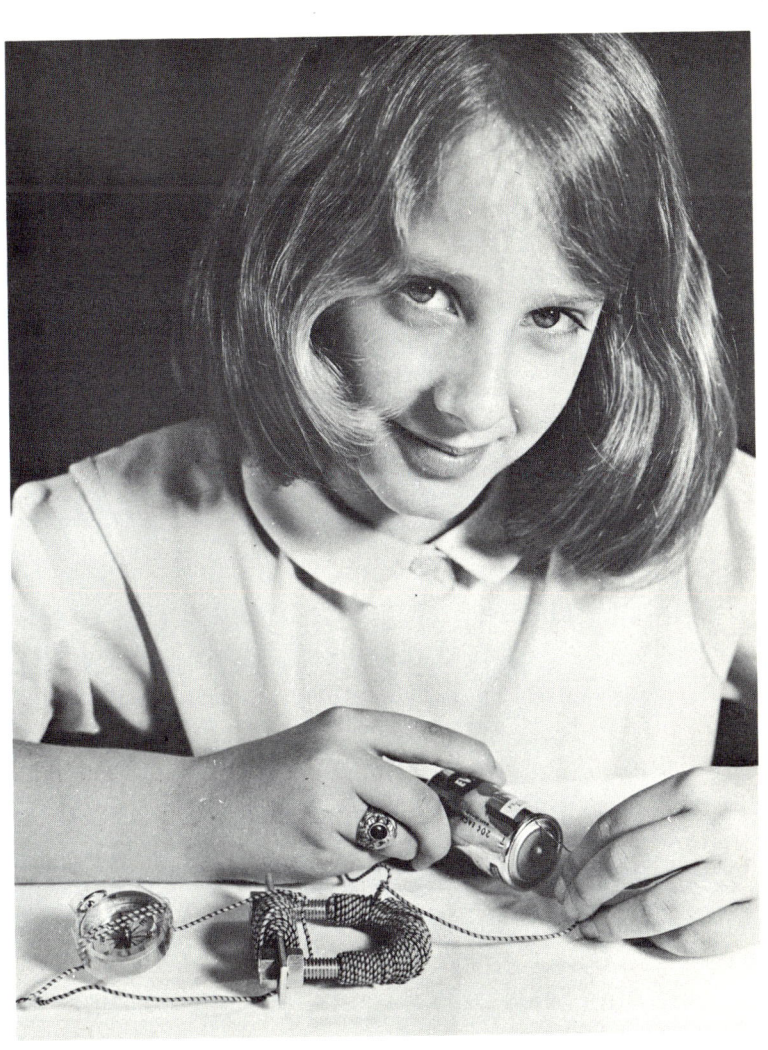

# William Thomson, Lord Kelvin
## 1824-1907

William Thomson was an infant prodigy. His father was a famous mathematician and university professor. Young William attended his lectures and understood them when he was only eight years old. He entered the University of Glasgow at eleven, finishing second in his class. While still in his teens he wrote his first learned paper. It was good enough to be read before the Royal Society of Edinburgh, but the august gentlemen of the Royal Society could not let themselves be lectured by a mere boy. An elderly man read young William's paper before the distinguished group.

William and his father were both professors at the same time for many years, the father a professor of mathematics and the son a professor of science, which was then called "natural philosophy." During the more than fifty years William held the chair in science he introduced a new technique: teaching in the laboratory as well as in the lecture hall. Since then the laboratory has been a necessary part of the teaching of science.

He first drew attention and much criticism to himself in 1846 by estimating the age of the earth at a hundred million years. He believed that the earth came out of the sun and took that long to cool.

He was always interested in heat. He proposed an absolute temperature scale in which zero would be that temperature at which all motion of molecules ceased. There could be no lower temperature than that. And he set that temperature at 273 degrees Centigrade below zero. The scale was adopted and is used today almost exactly as Kelvin invented it. Its temperatures are read as "degrees Kelvin."

He was associated with Cyrus W. Field, an American financier who was trying to send messages across the Atlantic by means of an undersea cable. He invented several improvements in the cable, and built measuring instruments that made the venture successful.

Signals from the cable were so weak that they would not operate the usual telegraph receiving instruments. Thomson built a galvanometer with a mirror attached to reflect a small beam of light. The currents from the cable could move the mirror slightly, and the slight motion of the mirror caused a large movement of the light beam, a movement that could be read and interpreted. Such mirror galvanometers are still in use.

Not satisfied, he went on to devise an improvement, the "syphon recorder." In this, a small glass tube floated with one end in ink and the other end pointing to a ribbon of paper moved by machinery. Electric attraction of the ink to the paper caused tiny droplets of ink to spurt out of the tube onto the paper, making a wavy line that could be read as dots and dashes. The tube never touched the paper, so there was no friction for the weak currents to overcome.

The name "Kelvin" was bestowed upon Thomson in 1892, by Queen Victoria, when he was made Baron Kelvin of Largs. This honor was given for his success in developing the successful cable. The name was taken from the Kelvin River near Glasgow. The title carried with it much wealth, and Kelvin lived his last year in happiness with his wife on his estates.

He is also remembered as being the one man who did more than anyone else to introduce Bell's telephone in Great Britain.

With James P. Joule (1818–1889) he developed the systems of cooling that make possible the liquefying of gases. In this way he contributed to our present space effort, since many rocket fuels require liquid oxygen for their combustion. He suggested a process of refrigeration based on the cooling of compressed air or other compressed gases when they are allowed to expand. This is the principle of our air-conditioning systems, wherein a liquid boils and expands under reduced pressure, then condenses again under increased pressure.

His patents up to the year 1900 numbered fifty-six, in the fields of telegraphy, compass and navigation devices, dynamos and electric lamps, electric measuring instruments, electrolytic production of alkali, and valves for fluids.

To the last he was interested in all new ideas in science, one of them being electrons, which he called "electrions."

In a paper read before the Glasgow Philosophical Society he told of the oscillations of a Leyden jar discharge, an idea followed by James Clark Maxwell (1831–1879) and Heinrich Hertz (1857–1894) in laying the foundations of radio. He verified the prediction of his brother, Professor James Thomson, that the melting point of ice is lowered by pressure.

In 1859 he studied and talked about atmospheric electricity. In this or the following year he invented the water-dropping electric machine, described in this book, which he called his "water drop collector."

A fall on the ice crippled him in the winter of 1860-1861, and he walked with a limp the rest of his life. He was always interested in the sea, owned a yacht, and improved the mariner's compass and other seagoing instruments.

But his latter years were not years of scientific brilliance as were his early and middle years. Although he served as President of the Royal Society from 1890 to 1894, he had begun to veer toward the eccentric with the conclusion that physics had advanced as far as it could go, that no further great discoveries would be made. This was about as wrong as any man could be.

He died in 1907, at the age of eighty-four, and left no children.

Lord Kelvin's brother, Professor James Thomson, predicted that it would be proved that the melting point of ice is lowered by pressure. Kelvin demonstrated this. Any pupil can perform an experiment to prove it today.

Get a fine wire—the kind furnace installers use to hold up hot air pipes is good—and attach a brick to both ends of it. Bring the middle of the wire up through a slot in a board and hang it over an ice cube.

Pressure of the wire will melt its way through the cube. A tricky feature of this experiment is that the water will freeze again on top of the wire, leaving the ice cube frozen together as before.

Kelvin's electric machine was not his greatest scientific contribution, but it is probably the most unbelievable yet simplest of all scientific devices. It can be built easily with almost no expense, and by means of its little drops of water it can produce more than 2,000 volts.

*A* and *B* are small juice cans, with both ends cut out. *C* and *D* are metal coffee cans, with only the top removed. They must hold water. The large can at the top is the water reservoir, from which tap water flows down through two rubber hoses.

Clamps to control the flow of water may be made from clothespins of the spring type, with a small wooden wedge in each for adjusting the flow. The paraffin blocks shown under cans *C* and *D* are the usual household variety, and are necessary for insulation. Without them or an equally good insulator, the machine cannot operate.

The neon lamp is a GE-NE51, which can be bought for about thirty cents from a radio or electronics store. A flashlight bulb will not work. The wires can be coat-hanger wires, and may be soldered to the cans or simply clamped around them with pliers. Two medicine droppers on the ends of the hoses are good but not necessary.

Cans *A* and *D* are connected by wires, and cans *B* and *C* are connected the same way. As the drops of water fall into the large cans a voltage is built up between the two sets of cans with their connecting wires. The drops must form inside the small cans and drop into the large cans.

To explain the operation of the machine we must assume that a small voltage difference would always exist between two objects insulated from each other. Suppose there is a small negative charge, which means a larger number of electrons, in cans $A$ and $D$ than in cans $B$ and $C$ at the start of experiment.

The voltage difference may be accounted for in a number of ways: a static charge on nearby clothing, a charge on the surface of the paraffin, a breeze that may be blowing slightly on one of the cans, or perhaps cosmic rays.

The drop forming in can $A$ will be in an electric field which will repel electrons. The drop will thus have a positive charge, slight though it be.

When the drop on the left breaks and falls it will carry its positive charge down into the large can on the left, which is connected by the wire to the small can $B$ on the right, and cause the drop forming in that can to become more negative.

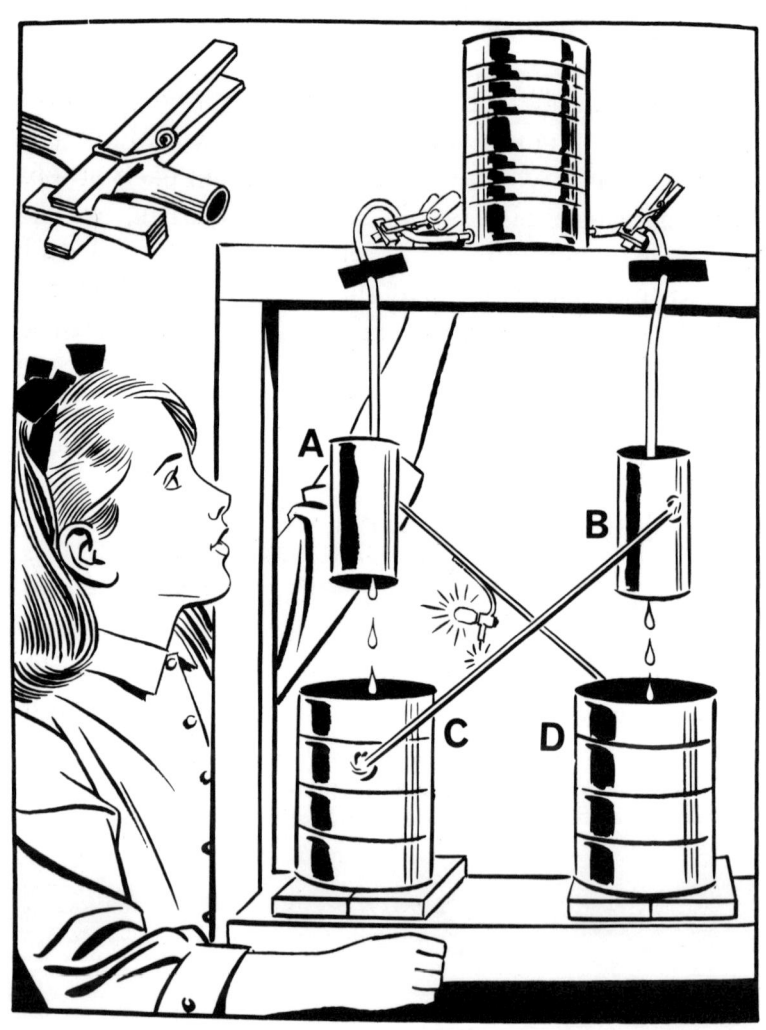

## Antoine Henri Becquerel
## 1852-1908

It is perhaps difficult to imagine that a great milestone in the development of modern atomic energy dates back to the days of Henri Becquerel, but it was through him that radioactivity was discovered.

He was born in Paris, into a family of scientists. Both his father and grandfather held the chair of physics in the Paris Museum of Natural History. At nineteen he entered the École Polytechnique, and at twenty-three published his first scientific paper on light and magnetism. In 1878 he became assistant at the Paris Museum where his father was professor of physics, on whose death Henri succeeded to the chair held in so distinguished a manner by his forebears.

In 1895 Wilhelm Konrad Roentgen (1845–1923) discovered X rays, the same year that Tesla, in America, was experimenting with them. Roentgen's discovery was widely publicized and created much excitement in the scientific community. Scientists began to investigate the phenomenon, and Becquerel was particularly intrigued by the fact that the newly discovered rays would make certain substances glow, or fluoresce. He wondered whether phosphorescent minerals could give off X rays, and began his experiments, trying many substances, including potassium uranyl sulphate. Quite by accident he discovered that the crystals containing uranium gave off a radiation that would affect a photographic plate wrapped in black paper, without exposure to light and without phosphorescence. He tried other uranium compounds, and found that all of them had the same mysterious property.

He had discovered radioactivity.

He observed that of all the uranium-bearing ores, pitchblende from Joachimsthal, Austria, was the strongest in radioactivity, and suggested to Marie Curie (1867–1934) that perhaps a thorough study of the pitchblende would disclose an element much more radioactive than uranium. This led to the discovery by Mme. Curie and her husband, Pierre, (1859–1906), of radium. In 1903 Becquerel and the Curies were awarded jointly the Nobel prize in physics for this discovery.

Becquerel made other important discoveries in science, mainly in light. He investigated polarization, the absorption of light by crystals, fluorescence, and phosphorescence.

It is easy to duplicate the experiment that led to the discovery of radiation. Get an old luminous watch or clock dial, no matter how battered, as long as it has the luminous numerals on it. Wrap a photographic film in black paper in the dark, so that no light gets to it, place the luminous numerals on the paper, and leave them overnight or for twenty-four hours. Develop the film. The film will have been fogged by the radiation coming from the clock face through the paper. The outline of the numerals will be seen on the film.

The radiation consists of alpha particles, which are stopped by the paper, beta particles which may go through thin paper, and gamma rays, which penetrate paper or even thin metals.

Luminous paint from the old watch and clock dials can be very dangerous if it enters the body, where it lodges in the bones. Never put such a dial in your mouth. Dispose of it after the experiment. Radiation from the dial through the air is harmless. Old dials contain radium or polonium, while the newer dials contain tritium and are relatively harmless.

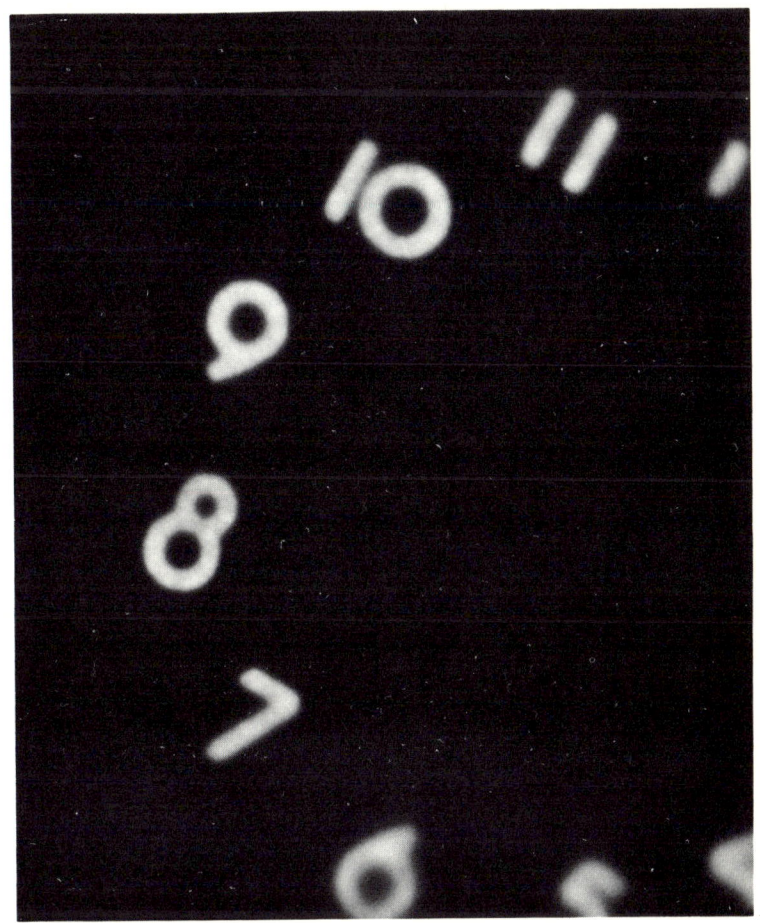

# Nikola Tesla
## 1856-1943

Nikola Tesla was born in 1856 in Smiljan, Croatia. His father was a minister of the church and a respected orator; his mother, although uneducated, was an inventor and a serious researcher in abnormal psychology. She conducted her psychological experiments on young Nikola and was often successful in transmitting her thoughts and projecting her wishes to him.

He started his scientific experiments at the age of five by making a blowgun from a tube he cut from cane. He experimented with a crossbow and a bug-powered motor. He built a water wheel from a disk cut from a log and was impressed with the possibilities of harnessing the power of rivers as he watched his tiny wheel develop power in the brook.

He attended the village school until, in 1863, his family moved to Gospic. After graduation from the Realgymnasium in 1870 he went on to more advanced studies at Karlstadt Graz, Austria, and attended the University of Prague.

Tesla was intensely interested in Alexander Graham Bell's new telephone invention and took charge of the first exchange in Budapest. He invented an improvement which he called a "repeater," a device which was the forerunner of our present loudspeaker.

His attention was drawn to the problem of solving the alternating current principle in electricity, for he was convinced that this was the only way in which the blessings of electricity could be made available to large numbers of people.

While working for the Continental Edison Company in Paris, he built the first induction motor. Although he introduced many improvements for this organization, his greatness was not recognized. He then decided to come to America. A letter of introduction resulted in a job with Thomas Edison at $18 per week. Before long Tesla suggested many improvements which resulted in vast savings. He was promised a bonus of $50,0000 if his research could be put to use. It was, but Edison went back on his promise and Tesla quit, feeling crushed and disappointed. For a time he worked as a ditch digger at $2 per day.

He met George Westinghouse, a wealthy inventor and financier, who after hearing Tesla recount his ideas and inventions, offered to finance the construction of models and gave him a million dollars for his patents and a royalty for their use. He formed the Tesla Electric Company and envisioned research which would give the great blessing of alternating current to the world.

At this time direct current was in universal use, but it had limitations and required a separate dynamo for each square mile of territory served and huge quantities of copper for wires. With Tesla's alternating current system, the voltage would be stepped up and the amperage lowered, and since wire size is determined by the amperage carried, the power could be sent over long distances on smaller wires with transformers to adjust the voltage and amperage.

Edison was worried by the competition Tesla was developing and called for drastic measures to forestall it, since his company had heavy investments in the direct current system. The great battle in the history of electricity commenced with Edison and his backers claiming that alternating current was much more dangerous than his direct current. Edison's campaign was being waged in a not too ethical fashion, and so Tesla and his backers began to employ arguments that were not altogether true. Tesla called in newspaper reporters and held them spellbound as he allowed high-voltage current from "Tesla coils" to flow over his body, lighting lamps and even melting wires. He won his point.

He went on to invent diathermy for medical use and built successful arc lights to replace gas for street lighting.

In 1889 he became an American citizen and moved to Colorado where he built the largest Tesla coil of all time. Although the coil worked perfectly at first, it suddenly went dead—the power went off. Power for operating the giant transformer came from Colorado Springs, and when the high voltage was being produced, some of it wandered down the transmission line and burned out the generator. Tesla abandoned the project and returned to New York.

He developed plans and directed the work for harnessing the power of Niagara Falls. He had ideas for a broadcasting laboratory, for television, but not being a businessman, he was always in financial trouble. He never bothered to collect the vast wealth due on his patents.

He died alone in a hotel room on January 7, 1943. The tragedy of Tesla's life was that he never recorded all his brilliant ideas and research. He is remembered mainly for his valuable contribution to mankind: his alternating current systems and motors.

Tesla's induction motor principle can be illustrated with the simple experiment shown here.

A permanent magnet—a strong one—is suspended on a string so that if the string is twisted the magnet will turn rapidly as the string untwists. An aluminum lid from a salt shaker is held under the magnet, without touching it. As the magnet turns, electric currents are induced in the aluminum, in such a way that they produce magnetic fields that repel and attract the fields of the permanent magnet so as to produce the turning motion in the lid.

In the photo the lid is balanced on a pencil point, which rests in a slight dent in the cardboard liner inside the lid.

Should anyone suspect that air currents produced by the turning magnet can make the lid turn, a piece of paper or thin cardboard may be held between the magnet and the lid to block any air current. The magnetic lines of force penetrate the cardboard without difficulty, and the lid turns just as well.

In the motor the magnets do not turn, but are energized one after the other, producing the effect of a rotating magnetic field. This rotating field serves the same purpose as the rotating field from the turning magnet in the photo.

It is not difficult to build a small Tesla coil which will give 100,000 harmless volts. The materials needed are:

1 neon sign transformer, with one side of its secondary still good (this can be obtained from a sign shop), or else a furnace burner transformer, which will do as well.

1 cardboard tube, 2½ to 3 inches in diameter, about a foot long.

Magnet wire, size 25 to 32. The author used 520 feet of number 28.

12 feet of copper ribbon or large size (10 gauge) copper wire, either insulated or bare.

1 extension cord and plug attached to the neon transformer.

12 feet of No. 12 insulated wire for coils and connections.

7 small battery or alligator clips from auto or electronics store.

1 copper bowl or ball, preferably slightly larger than tube diameter. (The outfit will work without this.)

4 spring clothespins.

28 pieces of single strength window glass, 5 by 8 inches.

27 pieces of kitchen foil, 3 by 8 inches.

Tape, shellac, pieces of ¾-inch wood (dry), pliers, knife, saw, drill, screwdriver, and other tools found in the home workshop.

Last but important, a good assistant.

A word of caution is necessary, even before the construction begins. Current from a lamp cord, which is usually 120 volts, is deadly. The high voltage from the neon or furnace transformer can be dangerous if the rating of the transformer is more than 40 milliamps (Ma.) The voltage of the transformer secondary can be from 3,000 to 12,000, but the Ma. rating determines the danger. The voltage from the Tesla secondary, which should be as high as 100,000 volts, is harmless.

Wind the magnet wire on the cardboard tube in one layer. It is good to shellac the tube both before and after the winding. Wind the heavy ribbon or wire in a spiral shape, on wood supports, as shown. Make the condenser with window glass and foil, as shown, so that alternate pieces of foil extend at alternate ends of the glass.

The two coils and spark gaps mounted on plywood are designed to prevent the easy wandering of the high frequency current back into the neon transformer, where it could burn out the secondary coil there. The author's large Tesla coil employs capacitors for this purpose.

The spark gap shown on one leg of the spiral support is quite important. Set it so that it is wide. The wires should be just close enough together so that the spark will jump between them.

The author used a flower bowl, without its chain supports, for the top of the Tesla secondary. An alternate is a round copper ball obtained from a plumbing shop. A heavy wire support may be soldered to the ball, to hold it two inches above the top of the cardboard tube. The bowl, which is slightly larger than the tube, may rest on top of the tube.

This is a diagram of the small Tesla coil layout. *A* is the neon transformer, with a connection made to the good end and to the case. *B* is the protective device (which may be omitted). *C* is the condenser, *D* the spark gap, and *E* the Tesla transformer primary. *F* is the space for the Tesla secondary coil.

The connection from the spark gap to the center of the Tesla primary is stationary. The connection from the condenser to the Tesla primary is adjustable by means of an alligator clamp on the end of the wire.

Clothespins are used to clamp the wires to the ends of the foil at the condenser (page 150).

At upper left is a close-up of the instrument for protecting the neon transformer from high voltage that might wander back from the Tesla transformer to burn out coils. It consists of two spark gaps and two coils of 14-gauge house wire.

At upper right is the detail of construction of the condenser: alternate layers of glass and foil. Alternate foil layers extend from opposite ends of the glass.

At lower left is the detail of the support for the Tesla primary. Four of these are used. If copper ribbon is not easily obtainable, heavy wire, about 10-gauge, may be used. It may be wound around an oatmeal box instead of the wood supports.

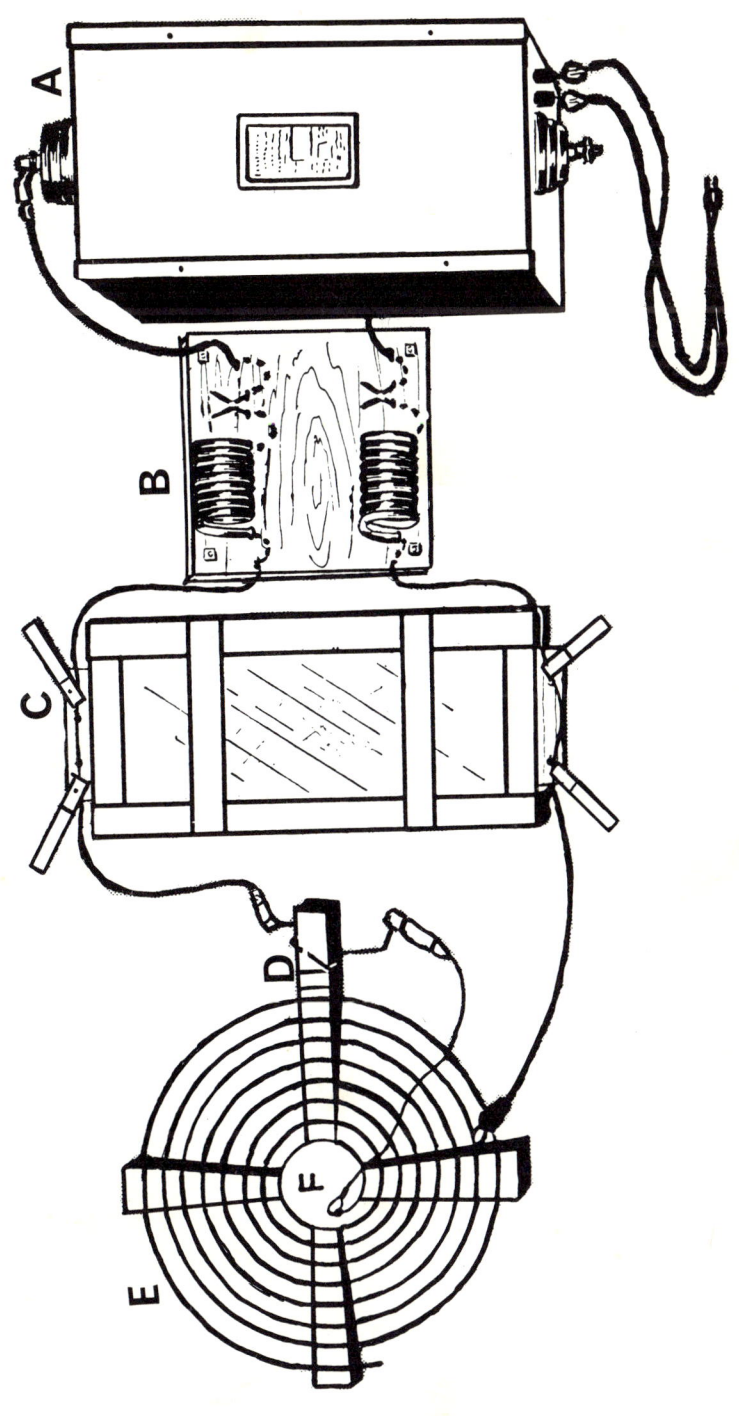

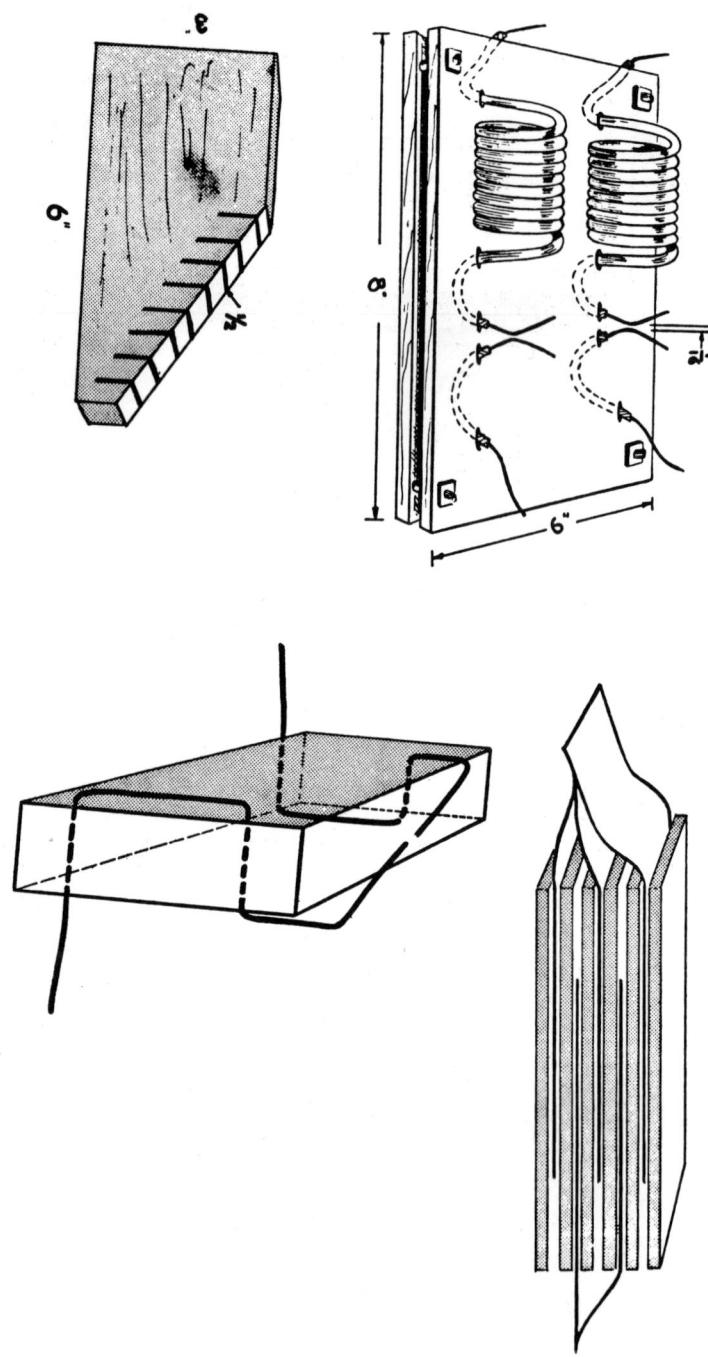

The spark gap arrangement is shown at lower right. It may, in a small Tesla coil, consist only of two heavy copper wires with an air gap between.

Here the construction is shown almost complete. The condenser is being assembled with alternate layers of glass and foil. The clothespins will be used to clamp the ends of the foil to the wires.

(page 153)

The spark from the small Tesla coil will light a neon sign or fluorescent tube. It is necessary that someone turn the switch on and off, while someone else holds the tube. A burned-out tube will light, as long as the gas remains in it.

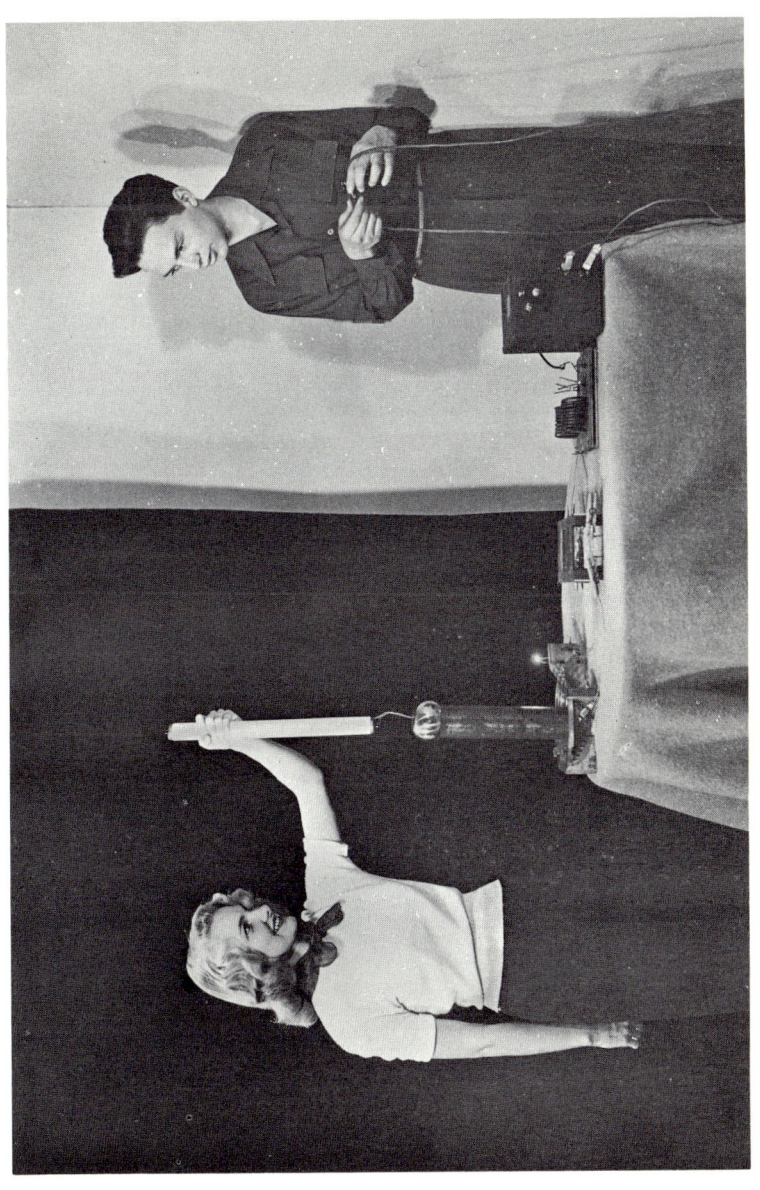

The entire lower part of the Tesla coil can be covered with a wooden case, with only the Tesla secondary sticking up through a hole. This would make for greater safety in case a small child was inclined to touch some of the parts that could give a painful shock. In the photo a girl is holding a table knife, allowing the spark to hit the end of it.

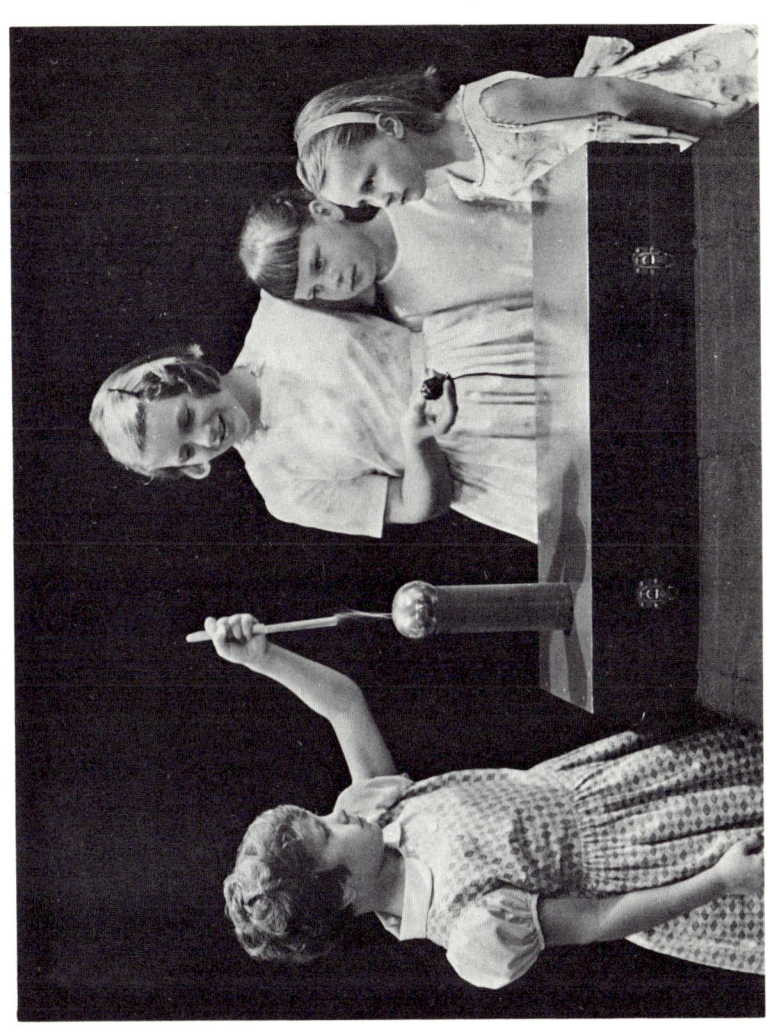

This is the schematic diagram of the author's large Tesla coil.

A and B are small capacitors used to protect the windings of transformer C from high voltages that may wander back from the Tesla secondary H and cause shortages and burn-outs. They are rated at 1 microfarad (mf or MFD) at 1,000 volts, and drain wandering high-frequency currents harmlessly to ground.

Sw is the foot switch in the 120-volt line.

C is the transformer used to step up the 120 volts to 12,000 volts.

D is a resistor, rated at 50 watts and 100 ohms, used to limit the output of the transformer C. Too great a drain on the transformer could burn out its secondary.

E is the series of spark gaps.

F and F are two condensers, 12,000 volts and .02 microfarads.

G is the Tesla primary, and H is the secondary. G consists of 10 turns of copper tubing 5 inches high and 14 inches in diameter. H consists of 430 turns of 19-gauge wire on a 7-inch bakelite tube 31 inches tall.

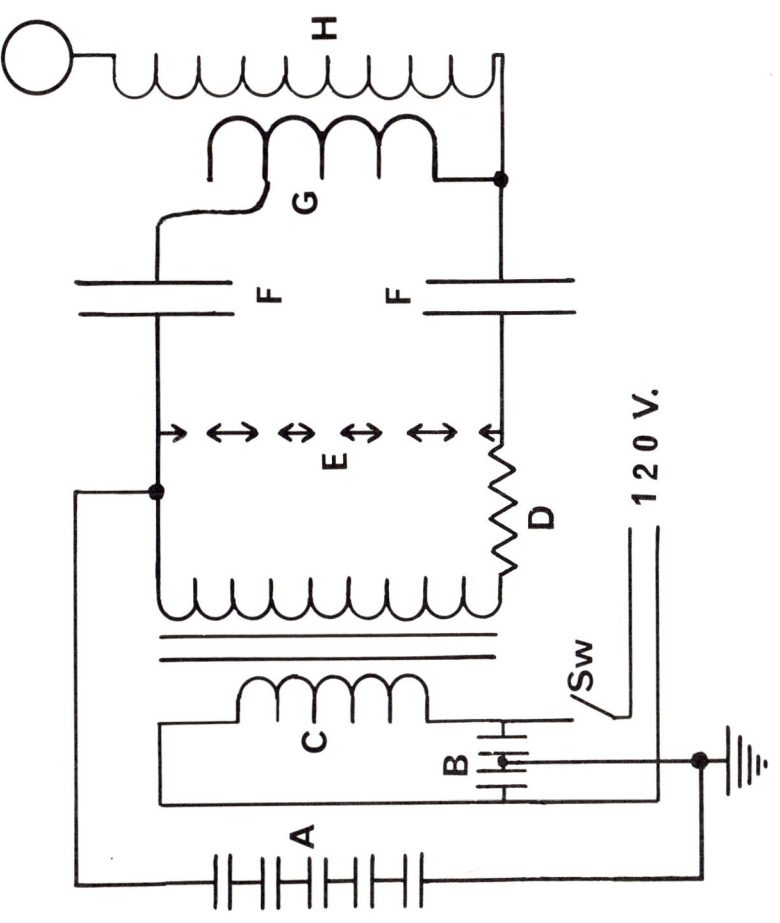

Demonstrations as spectacular as this may be performed with the author's large Tesla coil. The girl is shown standing on the Tesla secondary in bare feet, with the electricity flowing up her body. Thimbles on her fingers protect them from burns. Each thimble is connected with a wire to the copper band on each wrist. This prevents shock in the wrists. The current does not affect the watch she is wearing.

It was demonstrations such as this that Tesla used to promote his alternating current system and refute claims of danger advanced by Edison. Actually, low frequency alternating current is as dangerous as direct current, and in some cases more so. Tesla did not point this out, and so he won his point and was able to give the world cheap electric power.

# Index

## A

Acceleration, laws of, 28
Aeronautics, 65
Agriculture, 65, 69
Air conditioner, 16
Airplane, 54, 55, 56
Air pressure, 35, 56, 58, 60
Alexander the Great, 1
Alkali, production of, 128
Alpha particles, 137
Alternating current system, 142, 143
American Philosophical Society, 69
Ammonia, 78
Ammonium chloride, 91
Ampere, 118
Apple, 44
Archimedes, 6
   screw, 10
   photo, 11
Aristotle 1, 24, 26
   photo, 5
Armature, 65
Armonica, 68
Astronomy, 64
Atmosphere, pressure of, 35, 36
   photo, 37

## B

Ball and roller bearings, 20
   photo, 21
Ball, table tennis, 60, 62
   tennis, 52
Balloon, Franklin's comment, 68
   rubber, 48
Battery, 65, 91, 120, 122
Bearings, roller, 16

Becquerel, Antoine Henri, 135
   photo, 138, 139
Beethoven, Ludwig Von, composer, 68
Bell, Alexander Graham, inventor, 128, 141
Bernoulli, Daniel, 54
   experiments, 57, 59, 61, 63
   drawing, 61
   photos, 57, 59, 63
   theorem, 55
Beta particles, 137
Body, human, 19
   dissection, 19
   bleeding, 99
   heart, 19
Bombs, 16
Borgia, Cesare, Italian military leader, 19
Botany, 65
Brewery, 76
Bridges, 16
Bubonic plague, 43

## C

Cable, Atlantic, 127
Caloric, 54
Can, 50
Candle, 79
Cannon, 16, 17
Capacitor, 65
Carbon dioxide, 76, 77, 95
Carbon monoxide, 78
Catapults, 18
Centrifugal force, 44
Chemistry, 64
Clock, 16, 29
Cohesion, 28
Compass, mariner's, 129

Condenser, 65
Conductor, electrical, 65
Continental Edison Company, 141
Copernicus, Nicholas, Polish astronomer, 27, 28
Copying machines, electrostatic, 64, 70
Crown of cups, 82
Crystals, 39, 109, 136
Curie, Marie and Pierre, French physicists, 136

## D

D'Alibard, Thomas-François, French scientist, 67
Da Vinci, Leonardo, 16
  Caterina, 17
  Horse, bronze, 18
  Last Supper, painting, 18
  photos, 21, 22
  Piero, 17
Davy, Sir Humphry, English scientist, 108, 109, 110
Diggers, mechanical, 16
Dime, to make battery, 91
Direct current system, 141
"Dissenters", religious group, 76
Drive, variable speed, 16

## E

Earth, age of, 127
Edison, Thomas, 141, 142
Electrical shock, 65
Electric fluid, 65
  lamp, 128
Electrician, 65
Electricity, 65, 109, 111, 118
  "animal", 82
  atmospheric, 129
  generating principle, 107
  house current danger, 147
  "taste" of, 82, 84
  photo, 85
Electromagnet, 117

Electrophorus, 81, 86, 88
  photo, 87, 89
Energy conduction, 55
Erector wheels, 48
Erie Canal, 117
Ethnology, 65
Euclid, Greek mathematician, 25
Evaporation, 55
Eye glasses, 69

## F

Falling bodies, laws of, 28, 32
  drawing, 33
Faraday, Michael, 107, 117
  photos, 112, 113, 114
Field, Cyrus W., American financier, 127
Fluid, 55, 128
Fluorescence, 136
Fog signals, 109
Foil, kitchen, 91
Francis I, King of France, 19
Franklin, Benjamin, 64, 77
  kite, 66, 67
  photos, 71, 73, 75
Frog's legs experiment, 81, 82
Funnel, 60

## G

Galileo Galilei, 24, 34
  photos, 31, 33
  water balance, 26
Galvani, Luigi, 81, 82
Galvanometer, 111, 127
  photos, 112, 113
Gamma rays, 137
Gases, 55
Geology, 64
Glasgow Philosophical Society, 128
Glass harmonica, 68
Gluck, Christoph, composer, 68
Gravity, 44, 109
Guericke, Otto von, 34
  photo, 37

Gulf Stream, 68
Guns, machine, 16

## H

Heat, 54, 68
Heat conduction, 68, 74
   photo, 75
Helicopter, 16
Henry, a measure of inductance, 118
Henry, Joseph, 115
   drawings, 121, 124
   photos, 122, 125
Henry, William, 93
   Henry's law, 93
   photo, 96
Hertz, Heinrich Rudolph, German physicist, 118, 128
Hiero, King, 6
History, 65
Hooke, Robert, 38
   Hooke's law, 40, 41
   photo, 42
Horses, 35
Hose, garden, 62
Hull, of ship, 16
Hydrography, 65
Hydrostatics, 28
Hygiene, 65

## I

Induction, electrical, 81
Induction motor principle, 144
   drawing, 145
International Electrical Congress, 83
Inquisition, 28

## J

Jet propulsion, 48
Joule, James P., English physicist, 128
Journal of Medicine, 98
Jupiter, 27

## K

Kelvin, Lord, (William Thompson), 126
   drawing, 134
   electric machine, 132, 133
   photo, 131
   regelation experiment, 130
   temperature scale, 127
Kepler, Johannes, German astronomer, 2

## L

Ladders, 17
Laënnec, René Théophile Hyacinthe, 97
   photos, 101, 103, 105, 106
Leibnitz, Baron Gottfried, 46
Lenses, 109
Lens grinder, 16
Leyden bottle (jar), 65, 128
Light, 39, 44, 45, 46, 69
   absorption, 69, 72
   photo, 73
Lightning, 65, 66, 67
   rod, 67
Lippershey, Hans, Dutch spectacle-maker, 27
Locks, canal, 16
Luminous dial, 137

## M

Magdeburg hemispheres, 34, 35, 36
   photo, 37
Magnet, 107, 109, 111
   photo, 114
Magnetic field, rotating, 144
Marcellus, 8
Mathematics, 65
Maxwell, James Clerk, Scottish physicist, 128
Medicine, 65
Meteorology, 64, 69
Milky Way, 27

Mining, 17
Moats, draining of, 17
Molecules, 55
Moon, 27, 39, 44
Moons of Jupiter, 27
Morse, Samuel F. B., inventor, 117
Motor, electric, 118, 120
   drawing, 121
   photo, 122
Mozart, Wolfgang A., composer, 68
Musical glasses, 68

### N

Nail, 50
Napoleon, (Bonaparte), 83
Nature, cycle of, 77, 79
   photo, 80
Navigation, 65
Neon sign transformer, 146
Newton, Sir Isaac, 43
   drawing, 51
   laws of motion, 28, 45
   photos, 47, 48, 49, 53
Nitric oxide, 78
Nitrogen, 78

### O

Ocean current flow, 68
Oils, 109
Oscillation, 25
Osmosis, 55
Oxygen, discovery of, 77
   liquid, 128

### P

Paleontology, 65
Parachute, 16, 20
   photo, 23
Paraffin, 91
Pascal, Blaise, French scientist, 34
Pencils, 52

Pendulum, 25, 30
   drawing, 31
Peregrinus, Petrus, 12
   photos, 14, 15
"Perpetual motion", 12
Philosophy, 65
Phlogiston, 54
Phosphorescent minerals, 136
Photographic film, 137
Physics, 64
Pin, 58
Pisa, Leaning Tower, 24
   swinging lamp in cathedral, 25
Pitchblende, 136
Plank, as a sound conductor, 97, 98, 100
Plato, 1
Polarization of light, 136
Pole, magnetic, 13
Polonium, 137
Poor Richard, 67
Press, printing, 16
Priestley, Joseph, 76
   photo, 80
Printing, 65
Prism, 45, 46
Projector, 16
Psychological experiments, 140
Pulley system, 6, 16
Pump, 16, 25
   air, 34

### R

Radio, 118, 128
Radioactivity, 135, 136, 137
   photos, 138, 139
Rainbow, 46
   photo, 47
Rays, alpha, beta, and gamma, 137
Record, phonograph, 70, 86, 87, 88, 89, 90
Refrigeration, 128
Resistance, air, 32
Richmann, G. W., Swedish physicist, 66

Rockets, space, 45
Roentgen, Wilhelm Konrad, German physicist, 135
Romans, 8
Royal Institution, 109
Royal Society, 40, 45, 69, 77, 82, 83, 93, 94, 129
Rumford, Count (Benjamin Thompson), 55

S

Salt, 91
Saw, power, 16
"Science for You", newspaper column, 48
Seesaw, 97
Seismology, 64
Sforza, Ludovico, ruler of Milan, 17
Shelburne, Lord, a scholar, 77
"Stillman's Journal", 118
Smithsonian Institution, 118
Soda straws, 52
Soft drink, 95
 industry, 76
Solar system, 27
Sound, 97, 98, 99, 100, 102
Spool, thread, 58
Stage, revolving, 16
Static electricity, 70, 86, 87, 88, 89, 90
Stethoscope, 97, 98, 99, 100, 102, 104
 photos, 101, 103, 105, 106
Stove, Franklin, 67
Strings, 50
Sturgeon, William, English physicist, 117
Submarines, 16
Sulphur dioxide, 78
Sun, 27

T

Telegraph relay, 117
Telephone, 118, 128, 141
Telescope, 45
Tesla Electric Company, 141
Tesla, Nikola, 140
 coils, 142, 146-148, 151, 154, 156, 158
 drawings, 145, 149, 150, 157
 photos, 152, 153, 155, 159
Thermometer, 55
Thompson, Benjamin, (Count Rumford), 55
Thomson, Professor James, 128
Thomson, William (see Kelvin, Lord)
Torricelli, Evangelista, Italian physicist, 34
Transformer, Henry's first, 123
 drawing, 124
 photo, 125
Tritium, 137
Tube, for experimental stethoscope, 104
 photos, 105, 106
Tuberculosis, 99
Tunneling, 18
Turbine engine, 16
Turkey, Franklin's, 67

U

Uranium, 136

V

Vacuum, 25, 34
Vacuum cleaner, 60
Ventilation problems, 109
Verrocchio, Andrea del, artist, 17
Vibrations, 55
Volt, 83, 118
Volta, Alessandro, 81
 photos, 85, 87, 89, 92
Voltaic pile, 82, 91, 108
 photo, 92

## W

Washington, George, President, 99
Watch, 38, 39
Water, 41, 62
Weather forecasting, 64, 69
Westinghouse, George, inventor, 141
Woods, W. M., scientist, 44
Wren, Christopher, 39

MAY 1 8 1970

94862

502. BROWN
8       SCIENCE TREASURES
BROWN

Date Due

**DISCARDED**

**South Huntington Public Library**
Huntington Station, New York

98